7 December 1941 — the stricken *West Virginia*, burning furiously during the attack on Pearl Harbor.

ACTION IN THE PACIFIC

As seen by US Navy photographers during World War 2

The most famous US battleship of the war, *Missouri*, on her way into Tokyo Bay, 27 August 1945, to accept the formal surrender of Japan.

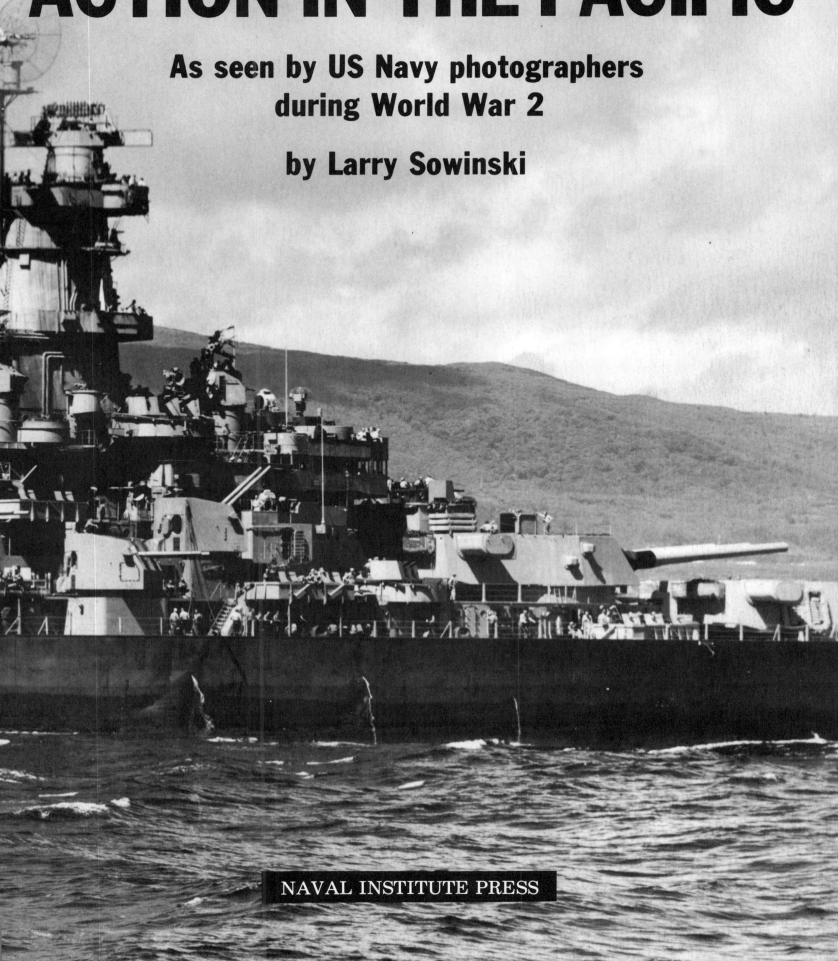

ACTION IN THE PACIFIC

As seen by US Navy photographers during World War 2

by Larry Sowinski

NAVAL INSTITUTE PRESS

After the victory parades,
after the flag waving,
after freedom has been preserved—
those who enjoy liberty are quick to forget.

This book is dedicated to an extraordinary American
who did not forget:
Mr Zachary Fisher of New York City,
Intrepid Museum Foundation
Veterans' Bedside Network
Honor America

© Lawrence Sowinski 1981
First published in 1981 by Conway Maritime Press Ltd, London

Published and distributed
in the United States of America and Canada
by the Naval Institute Press, Annapolis, Maryland 21402

Library of Congress Catalog Card No 81-83152

ISBN 0-87021-800-X

This edition is authorized for sale only in the United
States and its territories and possessions, and Canada.

Printed in Great Britain

FOREWORD

US Navy Combat Photographers took hundreds of thousands of pictures during World War 2. This book contains but a few hundred of them. For the most part, the photo coverage of the American naval war in the Pacific was adequate enough to arrange the pictures into chronological chapters. Each photograph has been briefly captioned. Some historical background had also been included for the purpose of presenting a more comprehensive overview.

However, it is not the purpose of *Action in the Pacific* to present another written account of the war at sea. On the contrary, the intention is to reproduce a comparatively large number of significant, as well as never-before-seen candid photographs. They were selected from the files of the US National Archives and the US Navy Photo Center (both are located in Washington, DC). A number of prints were also borrowed from private collections, but all are official US Navy, taken by Navy Photographers.

The Naval material stored in the National Archives is incredibly extensive, both in quantity and coverage, but there are a number of problems inherent in the Archives' vast holdings. Foremost is proper maintenance, compounded by restricted funding. Another problem is incomplete and occasionally inaccurate indexing, although the mammoth task of correcting and revising the filing and storage systems is an on-going project. Still another problem goes back directly to the source—the man who took the picture. At least a quarter of the photographs reproduced herein were captioned incorrectly. This is understandable once the conditions under which many pictures were taken are considered. It must be remembered that most Navy Photographers did not have extensive training in ship identification, which often resulted in faulty captions. During combat operations, photographers were more concerned about getting a decent picture without getting killed, than whether or not they were photographing the *Missouri* or her sistership, the *Wisconsin*.

The Archives Naval Still Photo Section is divided into two major categories, the BUSHIPS File and the BUAIR File (Bureau of Ships and Bureau of Aeronautics respectively). The BUSHIPS' photographs number over 150,000 negatives, generally covering the period from 1900 to 1970. For the most part, they are strictly ship's portraits, construction, and modification views. The file contains a number of magnificent close-ups which are now being reproduced in contemporary publications on a regular basis. The vast majority of BUSHIPS pictures were taken during World War 2.

Over one million pictures are in the BUAIR Files, which contain everything: combat operations, training, captured pictures, topographics, personnel, aircraft, ships, etc. Some overlapping into the BUSHIPS File is not uncommon, especially with regard to duplication of ship portraits. *Action in the Pacific*'s interest is limited to BUAIR's opera-tional photographs, taken in the Pacific during the Second World War.

Inaccurate captions presented a major difficulty with regard to the date the photo was taken, which was listed on each picture. The date could be off by days, weeks, months, or even years, and several pictures had no dates at all, while others were marked only with a date of receipt by BUAIR, although they had actually been taken earlier. Faulty dates are not a problem if the picture represents a period which can be verified through other sources (ship's histories, battles, etc), but some difficulty was experienced with pictures of ships underway, especially if the subject had not received any refits. For example, the carrier *Hornet* (CV-12) served with the Fast Carrier Task Force for 16 months without a noticeable change in her appearance— except for weathering. On the other hand, her battle-scarred sistership, the *Intrepid* (CV-11), received two major refits and a minor refit during approximately the same period. As such, it was always easier to verify an *Intrepid* picture's date than it was to put several *Hornet* photographs into accurate time frames. In most cases the author was able to date unmarked photographs by studying the paint schemes and general appearance of the ships and aircraft in the picture, other ships in the formation, and by reviewing relevant operational logs. Photos taken by other ships in the same formation were also used as an aid to verify some dates.

Evidently a number of photographs were intended for press release because all dates, locations, and ship identifications were removed. They were replaced with no information captions such as "United States warships on patrol in the Pacific". This was particularly true of the early war period.

In most cases the Archives contain the original photos, which means that none of the ship's radars or hull numbers have been retouched out by the censor. A few photographs are of rather poor quality, or are scratched or otherwise damaged. Nevertheless, they have been included because they are unique.

Periodic reference will be made to black and white copies of color transparencies which have deteriorated to a monochromatic red. This condition is common to a large portion of the US Navy transparencies taken during World War 2, but it was decided to reproduce a number of them in black and white because they are now valueless as color photographs. This was particularly frustrating since some of the best World War 2 warship color transparencies have deteriorated to red, most notably, all of the color pictures taken by *Intrepid* during the Philippines Campaign. Well-balanced black and white copies were difficult to produce from red transparencies because all of the value variations were in gradations of red which tends to copy too black when reproduced in monochrome.

US Navy ships which were lost in action often had their names reassigned to new construction. While this is commonly understood by navy men, it is sometimes a cause for confusion among the general public. The simplest means of differentiating between same-named ships is by their hull numbers. This would have necessitated considerable repetition, it was decided to delete hull numbers and type designations from the black and white picture chapters. Type designation indicated the kind of vessel, and the hull number identified the individual ship. For example— *Enterprise*, CV-6, meant that the *Enterprise* was the sixth carrier (CV) authorized. It must be kept in mind that the *Lexington* CV-2, which was sunk at Coral Sea in May 1942 was not the same as the new *Lexington*, CV-16, whose service began in 1943. At the time of this book's publication, the *Lexington*, now designated as CVT-16 still serves in the United States Navy as a training carrier at Pensacola, Florida.

Victory in the Pacific was spearheaded by American aircraft carriers and submarines. The very nature of submarine warfare precluded any decent photographic documentation. On the other hand, carrier warfare demanded large numbers of support and screening ships operating in relatively close proximity. Many of the vessels carried a Photographer's Mate at one time or another during the war.

Some ships took a considerable number of pictures, some took only a few. Some ships were always being photographed while it seems as though others were never photographed during operations. The pictures within this book also reflect this pattern. As such, the majority of the photographs tend to feature a relatively small number of ships. This does not detract from the overall story for each chosen vessel played a significant role in the Battle for the Pacific. America's fast carriers were Japan's prime targets for destruction. Conversely, they were the photographer's favorite subject. This placed the camera in the thick of the action.

If one ship were to be chosen which contributed most significantly to the Pacific victory, it would have to be the venerable aircraft carrier USS *Enterprise*. The *Enterprise* heads a long list of superb ships, made great by the men who served aboard them. *Action in the Pacific* invites you to walk back in history, to join the men of the *Enterprise*, *Intrepid*, *Hornet*, *New Jersey*, *Yorktown*, *Missouri* and *Hancock* (to name just a few) as they fight their way across the Pacific. The legacy of the *Enterprise* continues long after her death at a New Jersey scrap yard. Her spirit lives on in men like Admiral Bill Martin, former Secretary of the Navy Edward Hidalgo, and former Assistant Secretary of the Navy Joseph Doyle. All are *Enterprise* men.

A fitting tribute to the 'Big E' will be installed in the Aircraft Carrier Hall aboard the USS *Intrepid*. On 13 August 1980, Secretary of the Navy Hidalgo signed the recommendation to Congress for the preservation of the *Intrepid*, the signing taking place 3 days before the carrier's 37th birthday. *Intrepid* will live on as a Sea-Air-Space Museum in New York City.

Larry Sowinski

ACKNOWLEDGEMENTS

It is most appropriate that this World War 2 photographic history of the US Navy's Pacific campaign is introduced by Admiral Martin. The following pages contain an extensive coverage of the aircraft carrier USS *Enterprise*. More than any other warship, the *Enterprise* was responsible for the victory in the Pacific, and as a young naval aviator aboard the 'Big E', Bill Martin actually helped to make this history.

After graduation from the US Naval Academy in 1934, Ensign Martin was assigned to the battleship *Idaho*. Four years later, he received his wings and reported to the carrier *Lexington*. In 1940, he became an instrument flight instructor, first at Pensacola and then at Corpus Christi.

Lieutenant Martin joined *Enterprise*'s Scouting Ten while the carrier was being repaired in the summer of 1942 (after the Battle of the Eastern Solomons). His service aboard the *Enterprise* included command of dive-bomber and torpedo-bomber squadrons and the US Navy's first Night Air Group—CVG(N)-90. It was Bill Martin's pioneer development of night and all-weather offensive operations, and his skillful demonstrations of their viability, which led to the *Enterprise*'s designation as Night Attack Carrier. Additional carriers were also assigned this duty, giving the Fast Carrier Force the capability of striking the Japanese around the clock. For his accomplishments, Bill Martin was awarded the Distinguished Service Medal—the US Navy's youngest and most junior recipient.

After the war, Commander Martin went to Pautuxent, as a test pilot and Director of the Tactical Test Division. Captain Martin then went back to sea as commanding officer of the aircraft carrier *Saipan*, followed by duties with the Chief of Naval Operations.

After promotion to Flag rank in 1958, Rear Admiral Martin's assignments varied from Commander of Carrier Division Two (the Navy's first Nuclear Task Force including the new *Enterprise*) to Assistant Chief of Naval Operations for Air.

In April 1967, Vice Admiral Martin took over command of the powerful Sixth Fleet in the Mediterranean. His last active duty assignment was Deputy Commander-in-Chief, Atlantic Fleet.

Bill Martin holds the record with a phenomenal 440 night carrier landings. After retirement in 1971, he has remained very active in promoting Naval Aviation through the Association of Naval Aviation, the National Air and Space Museum, and the USS *Intrepid* Museum Foundation.

All photographs are official US Navy.

The author wishes to express his appreciation for assistance received from Robert Carlisle (US Navy Photo Office), James Trimble (National Archives), Clarke Van Fleet (Naval Aviation History), Thomas Walkowiak (Floating Drydock) and Robert Morales (New York Shipcraft Guild).

CONTENTS

LTCDR William I Martin, USN on board the *Enterprise* in March 1943.

INTRODUCTION

VADM William I Martin, USN (Ret)

Many of the pictures in this book represent a very personal trip back in time for me. The busy flight decks, the large formations of aircraft, the controlled pandemonium of kamikaze attacks—contrasted against peaceful scenes of resting ships, have all been brought vividly back as though it were yesterday.

Some of the photographs were particularly disturbing because they hit very close to home. Cameras were able to capture sequences of battle-damaged planes as they crashed on their carriers and broke apart. The realization that the young men inside these aircraft were my contemporaries, some were very close friends, only serves to emphasize their loss, even though they had died decades ago. God had truly watched over me as He allowed me to survive several crashes on the flight deck and into the sea after my plane had been critically damaged by anti-aircraft fire.

Like so many men who fought the war, I rarely got to see more than that which occurred immediately around me and my carrier—the *Enterprise*.

While numerous books have talked extensively, and motion pictures have glamorized unrealistically, few attempts have been made to reproduce the immense pictorial record made by the United States Navy's Combat Photographers. They took hundreds of thousands of pictures during World War 2. Almost all of them were very candid. Therefore, their cameras were able to truly capture the beauty and vastness of the Pacific, the will and spirit of America under arms, and the sacrifice and horror of war.

Even though Larry Sowinski has selected the most unique and many never-before-seen photographs, he has not been able to give us a well-rounded and complete picture of the US Navy's operations in the Pacific. Some significant battles were not photographed—or if they were, the pictures did not survive. The World War 2 combat camera also had its limitations. Numerous actions were fought at night. This generally restricted photo coverage to the battle's aftermath, as was the case with so many South Pacific engagements.

Darkness also prohibited the photographing of continuous, 24-hour-a-day carrier operations. This late-war capability kept Japanese positions under constant and accurate attack. The effect was devastating to their morale, robbing them of much needed sleep and the opportunity to make repairs or to resupply.

Perhaps this book's most serious omission is the lack of photographs of the intensive submarine war which was waged against Japan's naval and merchant fleets. Here again the camera's limitations could not provide pictures in proportion to the US submarine's contributions.

American submarines fought history's only successful undersea campaign. Despite unreliable torpedoes, we were able to wreck havoc on Japan's war effort and its vital supply lines. It must be remembered that the Japanese went to war for the stated purpose of acquiring a secure and uninterrupted supply of raw materials, especially petroleum.

Instead, the flow of merchant ships from recently won possessions to the Japanese mainland was greatly hampered by an aggressive submarine campaign. Towards the end of 1944 her sea lanes were just about totally strangled. US subs roamed Japanese controlled waters almost at will, hunting and sinking targets of opportunity, both merchant and naval. The submarine campaign was complemented by the fast carrier forces which also roamed the Pacific, drawing away the enemy's ships and aircraft which were needed for their anti-submarine operations.

The overall result was disastrous for Japan. Production was eventually reduced to a standstill. Training had to be cut to the bare minimum. The lack of raw materials eliminated the possibility of building ships in sufficient numbers to replace losses. Less ships meant that even less raw materials could be delivered, to build even less ships, to replace even greater losses.

It was the carrier forces which enjoyed much of the combat photographer's attention. The fast carriers played a major role in attaining victory in the Pacific. Spearheaded by the large *Essex* class carriers, with their superior aircraft skillfully flown by daring pilots and aircrews, they wrested control of the Pacific away from the Japanese. Numerous enclosed pictures attest to this fact.

The photographs also accurately document the array of escort and support ships which were needed to protect and service the carriers. Combined into the Fast Carrier Task Force, these ships were able to move quickly and strike isolated strong points with overwhelming power.

All of the United States Navy's many ships and aircraft were only as good as the men who manned them. Their presence is integral to many of the photographs as we catch glimpses of sailors and airmen at work, at play, at war, and in death—the ultimate sacrifice for one's country. We owe those young men everything. We will not forget them.

VADM William I Martin US Navy (Ret)

1. Pearl Harbor
Destruction and Recovery

The United States was forced into World War 2 by the Japanese surprise attack on the Pearl Harbor Naval Base, in the Hawaiian Islands. Japan struck at 8am, on the quiet Sunday morning of 7 December 1941. The attackers had chosen this time because they believed that the base would be at its lowest point of readiness.

The main attack came in two waves from a combined total of over 350 aircraft, from 6 aircraft carriers escorted by 22 combat and support ships. This force was also supplemented by 30 submarines, which however, proved to be totally ineffective.

When the Japanese air squadrons arrived over Pearl, they found a good portion of the US Pacific Fleet. In the harbor

were 8 battleships, 9 cruisers, over 20 destroyers, 5 submarines and a number of repair and supply ships, oilers, and tenders—a total of 86 combat and service ships (plus smaller yard craft and auxiliaries).

The Japanese planes were ordered to destroy any carriers and battleships which happened to be in port, and all of the military aircraft on the island of Oahu. Fortunately for the Allied cause, none of the 3 US Pacific Fleet carriers was in the harbor. However, if the Japanese had waited another day or two, they might well have caught both the *Enterprise* and *Lexington*.

Initially, the attack (referred to as the Battle of Pearl Harbor by the Japanese) was a lopsided victory for them

and a total defeat for American arms. The Japanese left the once peaceful 'Pearl of the Pacific' covered with smoke and fire and in apparent ruin. While this was true of some of the ships, the oil storage tanks, docks and repair facilities were virtually undamaged. Even before the smoke had cleared, the base was made operational and continued to be absolutely essential to victory in the Pacific throughout the war.

It must be remembered that both the United States and Japan were at peace with each other at the time. The Japanese broke the peace by attacking without warning and while still maintaining diplomatic relations, although they had intended to declare war shortly before the air strike reached Pearl.

The Hawaiian Islands were one of those 'far away places' which lured young Americans to join the Navy for adventure, and to leave the country-wide economic depression behind them. Two US sailors take in a beautiful Hawaiian sunset and the graceful silhouettes of three aircraft carriers (left to right) *Ranger*, *Saratoga* and *Lexington*, anchored off Diamond Head during the 1930s.

Pearl at peace

1

2

3

In April 1940 the United States Fleet was moved to Pearl Harbor from its usual base on the US West Coast, and from February 1941 it was rechristened the Pacific Fleet. Ironically, this was a measure intended to deter the Japanese from aggressive action, but only served to make their surprise attack possible.

1 Units of the United States Pacific Fleet in 'Battleship Row', Pearl Harbor, during May 1935. The land mass at the lower right is Ford Island. The *Langley*, America's first aircraft carrier, is alongside the pier. The 4 battleships moored behind the carrier are: *New York* (outboard) and *Arizona* (inboard), followed by *Oklahoma* (outboard) and a *Maryland* class ship. Two additional battleships are tied up across the way, at the Ten Ten Dock in the Navy Yard. On the left is the *California* with a four-stacked *Omaha* class light cruiser across the pier. The flagship of the Pacific Fleet, the *Pennsylvania*, is moored in front of the *California*. This was the flagship's regular tie-up while in Pearl. However, on 7 December 1941, the *Pennsylvania* was in Drydock No 1 (shown in this picture holding another *Omaha*). The light cruiser *Helena* was at *Pennsylvania*'s berth and apparently was mistaken for the flagship by the attacking Japanese.

2 Another view of the battle force at Pearl, 3 years later (April 1938). Ford Island is in the foreground showing the newly constructed crew barracks, complete with tennis courts. The flagship of the Pacific Fleet's battle force, the *California*, is

directly behind the barracks, at the same mooring at which she would be sunk on 7 December 1941. The other ships in Battleship Row are: *Nevada, Oklahoma, New Mexico, Idaho* and *Arizona*, followed by two *Northampton* class heavy cruisers.

The Pacific Fleet comes to Pearl

3 The main battlefleet at Pearl on 3 May 1940. Normally stationed on the West Coast of the United States, the Pacific Fleet was moved to this forward base in the Hawaiian Islands because of the deteriorating situation in the Far East. This picture clearly demonstrates the misgivings expressed by a number of naval officers with the move to Pearl. The only access to the open sea is the narrow channel in the upper left of this photo. Even with a limited warning, it is obvious that only a handful of ships could get out. The bottleneck effect might well mean that ships would easily be sunk in the channel, thus closing the escape route and trapping the fleet inside.

Visible in this view are 10 battleships, 12 heavy cruisers and approximately 36 destroyers. Only one carrier, the *Yorktown*, is in port. Ford Island with its airstrip is in the center; Pearl City is on the peninsula above and to the right of Ford. The Navy Yard is left of Ford Island, with the Submarine Base just below the yard, across the Southeast Lock, with 18 black-painted subs visible. Several of the destroyers in the East Lock (right of Ford Island) are also painted black.

13

Preparations for war

1 By October 1941, all signs of the peacetime US Navy at Pearl Harbor are gone. The ships no longer wear the very light gray paint. It has been replaced by the menacing Measure 1 camouflage scheme (dark gray with light gray top masts). Both of the battleships shown are at the same moorings as they would be on the morning of 7 December: the *Arizona* (extreme left, next to Ford Island) would become the tomb for over 1,000 of her crew. The *Nevada*, just aft of *Arizona*, is wearing a fake bow wave, as is the *Northampton* class cruiser at the right. The purpose of the fake bow wave was to deceive enemy submarines as to the vessel's actual speed and thereby cause torpedo aiming miscalculations.

Narrow escape for *Enterprise*

2 At sea, the day before the attack on Pearl Harbor, the *Enterprise* and her escorts head back towards Hawaii after delivering 12 fighter aircraft to Wake Island. Another carrier group, built around the *Lexington*, was on a similar mission to Midway. The other Pacific Fleet carrier, *Saratoga*, was at San Diego.

3 The destroyer leader *Clark* refuels from the *Enterprise* on 6 December 1941. Although heavily armed with eight 5in low angle guns, these leaders were not as effective as other US destroyers which were armed with dual-purpose guns (for both surface and air action).

Day of infamy

'Air raid, Pearl Harbor—This is no drill.' The famous signal was made just before 8am on Sunday 7 December 1941. The first Japanese strike of some 190 planes concentrated on the capital ships in Battleship Row, leaving *Oklahoma* capsized, *Arizona* a total wreck, *Nevada* beached, *West Virginia* and *California* sunk, and *Maryland*, *Tennessee* and *Pennsylvania* damaged. The second strike of 170 planes met more opposition and was less effective, but by 9.45 when the final Japanese plane departed the Navy had lost over 2,000 killed and 700 wounded.

The sunk and burning *West Virginia*. She was one of the outboard ships in Battleship Row which took the brunt of the damage. The *West Virginia* was hit by 6 or 7 torpedoes (all on the portside) and 2 bombs, killing 105 of her crew, including her commanding officer. The inboard ship behind the *West Virginia* is the *Tennessee*.

15

The destroyer *Shaw* was high and dry in Floating Drydock No 2 on 7 December. The forward portion of the ship was hit in rapid succession by 3 bombs which ruptured her oil storage tanks and blasted flaming oil throughout the destroyer's forward compartments. This caused the *Shaw*'s forward magazines to explode.

Five subs were moored at the Submarine Piers during the attack. Crewmen manned everything from deck guns to rifles in an attempt to fight back. However, the capital ships were the primary Japanese targets. In the background, across the Southeast Lock, the Navy Yard appears to be a mass of confusion with cruisers getting up steam. The oiler passing through the Lock (on the right) is the *Neosho*, laden with highly volatile aviation gas. Her captain has just moved her out of harm's way—from between the burning *California* and capsized *Oklahoma* (in the middle of Battleship Row). The *Neosho* was the first ship to get underway during the attack.

The beached *Nevada*

Three incredible views of the beached *Nevada*. She was the only battleship to escape from Battleship Row during the attack. Once underway, the *Nevada* became the focal point of the Japanese attack. She was hit by a total of 6 bombs, 3 large holes were opened in her side and she burned fiercely. When it became obvious that she might be sunk in the channel and block the harbour, *Nevada* was beached off Hospital Point. Note the fires on the forecastle and the bow very low in the water. These pictures were taken after *Nevada* had been beached to prevent her from settling any lower in the water. Fifty of her crew were killed during the morning.

Battleship Row

The flagship of the Battle Force, Pacific Fleet, burns and lists. The *California* was hit by 2 torpedoes and 2 large bombs. These explosions ruptured full oil storage tanks and caused extensive fires. It must be remembered that all the ships in the harbor were opened up (watertight doors were open) allowing fires to spread and compartments to flood quickly. Canvas shade awnings also had to be removed to give the guns a clear field of fire. The burning ship in the background is the *West Virginia*.

1 The leading ship in Battleship Row, *California*, is surrounded by boats and yard craft. She remained afloat for 3 days but water continued to flood into the ship until she finally settled in the mud. The *California* lost 98 men killed in action.

2 Looking at the remainder of Battleship Row after the attack. On the right is the capsized hull of the *Oklahoma*. Her portside was hit by 4 torpedoes within 15 seconds. A fifth torpedo then hit her and she rolled over. Her tripod masts dug into the muddy bottom. She lost 415 of her crew. The *Maryland* inboard of the *Oklahoma* was lightly damaged by 2 bombs. The *West Virginia* and *Tennessee* are behind her. The cloud of smoke in the background is from the *Arizona*.

3 When the *West Virginia* sank in the mud, she pushed against the inboard *Tennessee*. This in turn, wedged the hapless *Tennessee* against the large cement mooring pilings. With the burning *West Virginia* alongside, and the water astern aflame with burning oil from the wrecked *Arizona*, the *Tennessee*'s captain tried to free his ship by getting underway, but it was useless. However, the prop wash kept the burning oil away, so her screws were kept turning. Hit by 2 bombs, she suffered only 5 killed.

3

Ford Island

1 This picture was taken on Ford Island, looking across at Drydock No 1 in the Navy Yard. The burning *Pennsylvania* is in the after portion of the dock (she had been hit by only one bomb during the attack). The pall of smoke at the forward part of the dock is coming from the destroyers *Cassin* and *Downes* which were hit by 3 bombs, whose explosion ignited oil, torpedo warheads and ammunition on both ships.

2 Catalina flying boats burn on Ford Island. All but one of the 69 Catalinas were destroyed or damaged. Another 7 were airborne and thus escaped. A total of 188 American aircraft were destroyed; almost all were caught on the ground. Only 30 of the 350 attacking Japanese aircraft were shot down.

The sunken *Arizona*

3
4 Two views of the stricken *Arizona*. Although an inboard ship, she was a total loss. The repair ship *Vestal* was outboard, but being comparatively shallow drafted, 2 torpedoes passed underneath her and exploded against *Arizona*. The *Vestal* was terribly damaged but managed to pull away and beach herself. The doomed *Arizona* was hit by approximately 8 large bombs which led to the explosion of the forward magazines. She continued to burn for several days. The stern of the *Tennessee* is at the right, covered with smoke. In the second view the forward tripod mast has collapsed onto the navigating bridge. Number 2 main turret is just visible above the water at the right. *Arizona* lost 1,103 men, approximately one-half of her entire complement.

One of the 2,008 Navy men killed in action on the morning of 7 December 1941. The Navy suffered most of the casualties out of a total of 2,335 killed.

Rescue operations

1 Close-up of rescue operations on the capsized *Oklahoma*. Holes were cut into the hull to free trapped men. Boats ran to and from the damaged vessels, carrying wounded men to the hospital ship *Solace* which was at anchor in the East Lock. The *Maryland* is obviously lightly damaged (she lost only 4 men). One of her spotter planes has been blown off of the No 3 turret catapult, leaving only the aircraft's float.

The wreck of the *Shaw*

2 Two views of the wrecked *Shaw* inside Floating Drydock No
3 2. The drydock also took 5 bombs and sank around the *Shaw*. The explosion of the forward magazine blew off the entire forward portion of the destroyer. Despite this tremendous damage, *Shaw* was rebuilt and went back to war.

2

3

23

Cleaning up

Although the Pacific Fleet had been hit hard, Pearl Harbor itself remained operational as a base, even immediately after the attack. The Japanese had ignored fuel oil tanks and repair facilities and these were particularly valuable in the massive cleaning up operation that followed. The most spectacular aspect of this was the raising of the sunken battleship *West Virginia* and capsized *Oklahoma*.

The *West Virginia* rests on the bottom of the harbor. The extensive damage to her port side is hidden by the yard craft alongside. The *Tennessee*, behind her, is afloat and riding high in the water, compared with the *West Virginia*. Although very similar in appearance, these two vessels were not sister-ships. The *West Virginia* was armed with eight 16in guns while the *Tennessee* carried twelve 14in guns.

1

1 Close-up of the *California* resting on the bottom. The main deck is under water. The scarred and paint-blistered ship's side is probably where she was torpedoed. *California* is carrying a large search radar antenna on the roof of the navigating bridge. Only 2 other battleships, the *West Virginia* and flagship *Pennsylvania*, were equipped with radar but none was operating at the time of the attack. Note the laundry hung out to dry.

Refloating the *California*

2 Bow-on view of the *California* undergoing salvage operations. **3** Another view of the salvaging of the *California*, with her bow now settled deeper into the mud. All 6 of the forward 14in guns have been removed, as has the cage mainmast. Both the sunken *West Virginia* and *Arizona* are in the background (over the oiler's bow, to the right of the *California*). The capsized hull of the *Oklahoma* is just visible, under the gun barrel of the forward mount on the vessel in the foreground.

1

2

Drydock No 1

3 The flooded Drydock No 1, showing the wrecked destroyers *Cassin* (DD-372) and *Downes*. Both have lost their masts. *Downes* has also lost her after funnel and suffered a direct hit on her bridge.

3

The remains of the *Arizona*

1 Two views of the wrecked and still burning *Arizona*. Her
2 smoke stack is entirely gone.

5

4

Salvaging the *West Virginia*

4 Close-up of the undamaged starboard side of the *West Virginia* undergoing salvage.

5 A close-up of the incredible amount of damage to the *West Virginia*'s port side hull, above the armor belt. The yard workers are standing on the remains of the forecastle deck. Most of the boat deck has been removed. The picture was taken in drydock on 14 June 1942.

This view of *West Virginia*, taken 2 days later, shows that much of the twisted decks visible on 14 June have been cut away.

Work continues on the *West Virginia* on 17 June 1942. Both of these photos clearly show the extent of the concentrated damage above the armor belt.

1

Total losses

1 Salvage work on the *Arizona* during December 1942. This close-up shows the armored conning tower, with all of the bridges and tripod foremast removed. It was finally decided not to refloat her.

2 The *Oklahoma* was righted thanks to a major engineering feat. Because of her extensive damage and the fact that, at best, she was totally obsolete, it was decided not to repair *Nevada*'s only sister-ship. While being towed to the mainland (to be scrapped), the *Oklahoma* sank.

2

1 The carrier *Saratoga* ties up at Pearl on 6 June 1942. She has just completed repairs at Puget Sound after being damaged by a Japanese torpedo. The *California* is undergoing repair at the Navy Yard in the background.

Nevada returned to service

The *Nevada* departs Pearl Harbor on 19 April 1942 after the completion of repairs. She was the first of the heavily damaged battleships to be returned to service.

Back to normal

Much effort went into the program of repairing the ships sunk or damaged in the Japanese attack. At the same time Pearl was also acting as a major forward base, repairing battle-damage as well as providing the more mundane back-up facilities.

Nearly a year after

1 Pearl Harbor on 8 August 1942. The effects of the sneak attack are still evident. On this side of Ford Island lies the capsized hull of the demilitarized battleship *Utah*. Directly across from *Utah*, on the other side of the island, lies the capsized *Oklahoma*. The *Pennsylvania* is tied to the mooring recently vacated by the refloated *California*. Just visible aft of the *Oklahoma* is a group of yard craft busy stripping off the *Arizona*'s superstructure. The battleship moored forward of the *Utah* is either the *Idaho* or *Mississippi*. Pearl City is in the foreground showing Pan Am's 'Philippine Clipper' docks and ramp (on the right).

2 Taken 10 days later on 18 August 1942 the *Pennsylvania* is still at her same mooring but she has been joined by *Colorado* (in front of her) and *Maryland* (behind the capsized *Utah* in the foreground). Additional battleships are visible in the Navy Yard at the top of the picture, including all 3 *New Mexico*s, the refloated *California* and the drydocked *West Virginia*. The harbor is empty of almost all other war-ships. The carriers, cruisers and destroyers are all in the South Pacific, in action off Guadalcanal. The fast pace of Pacific naval warfare has left the slow battleships behind. The conclusion must be made that the Japanese attack on Pearl Harbor was of little value to them in the long run since most of their priority targets remained in harbor for the first crucial year of the war regardless.

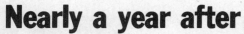

1

2

3 The brand new fast carrier, *Bunker Hill*, unloads men and equipment immediately upon arrival at Pearl Harbor, on 2 Oct 1943. The *Bunker Hill* had been preceded by 3 sistership ships beginning in May 1943 (*Essex*, *Lexington* and *Yorktown*).

4 The battleships *Pennsylvania* (BB-38) and *New Mexico* (BB-40) back at Pearl for a rest in December 1943 (between invasions). During November 1943 they supported the invasion of the Gilberts. In January and February 1944, they provided fire support for the invasion of the Marshalls. Pearl Harbor was less than half of the distance between the Marshall and Gilbert Island groups and the West Coast of the United States. It was the most valuable base in the Pacific and acted as a springboard for invasions until more advanced anchorages could be captured. By this date the *Pennsylvania* had been modernized by the addition of considerable anti-aircraft guns and the removal of the mainmast, to increase the arcs of AA fire.

Visitors to Pearl

American carrier losses were terrible during 1942. In March 1943 the Royal Navy's *Victorious* arrived at Pearl Harbor to serve as part of the US Fleet until the arrival of new carriers later in the Summer and Fall.

3

4

Submarine base

Four 'fleet boats' tied up at the Submarine Piers. Pearl Harbor remained invaluable as the main submarine operating base throughout the entire Pacific war.

2

3

1 Two views of the newly repaired *Saratoga* back at Pearl in
2 June 1945. She had been refitted at Puget Sound Navy Yard
on the West Coast and was now relegated to training duty
out of Pearl.

In for repairs

3 Battle-damaged ships used Pearl Harbor as a haven for both
temporary and permanent repairs. Shown is the *Hancock*
which had been hit by kamikazes (off Okinawa) during
April 1945. The Navy Yard had the carrier back in action by
June. Besides repairing the damage, extra anti-aircraft guns
were also added.

2. Hit and run
US Carrier Forces in Action, December 1941-June 1942

The period immediately following the attack on Pearl Harbor was filled with a seemingly endless chain of defeats for the Allies in the Pacific, and particularly for the United States. Prior to the attack, American naval strategy was built around a formidable battle-line, designed to operate as a homogeneous force with carriers, cruisers and destroyers in a supporting role. On 8 December 1941 5 units of that battle-line lay on the bottom of Battleship Row. To pursue the same tactics, with half the ships, would have meant the destruction of all of them at the hands of a numerically superior enemy battle-line.

The loss of battleships, which were too slow to operate within the new fast warfare concepts, did not greatly upset advocates of carrier aviation. However, unlike the US, only Japan now possessed a powerful and well balanced capability with numerous aircraft carriers supported by fast battleships with large guns (for either defense or offense). This enabled Admiral Yamamoto to pick and choose his targets while the Allies could only react, or be content to hit and run, and then hide.

Pearl Harbor was the most important US base in the Pacific, but while its loss was a distinct possibility, the loss of the Philippines was fast becoming a reality. The Japanese hoped to draw the remainder of the US Fleet into action, where it could be totally destroyed. Several Americans unwittingly called for just that, a glorious 'cavalry charge' to relieve Bataan. Instead, Admiral Nimitz, aware of his limited offensive capability, kept his ships close enough to Pearl to be able to counter any future attacks. While this did not make the Navy very popular in the first few months, it may well have shortened the war considerably.

Japan's striking Force, under Admiral Nagumo, was flushed with victory after victory. Soon the entire Japanese Navy became infected with extreme over-confidence. They had much to be confident about. Their losses had been negligible while they had sunk 7 battleships, 1 aircraft carrier, 4 heavy cruisers, 4 light cruisers and scores of destroyers and auxiliaries.

The US Navy, although always on the brink of disaster, managed to hold on and survive until reinforcements arrived, both from the Atlantic Fleet and from new construction. The political policies of the 1930s were to

Attempt to relieve Wake

The first carrier operation of the war was an abortive attempt to relieve the beseiged US Marine garrison on Wake Island. The *Enterprise* and *Lexington* were to act as cover for the *Saratoga* (loaded with Marine aircraft). Unfortunately, the island was over-run on 23 December 1941 while the relief force was still a day away. Shown are a line of *Gridley* class destroyers leaving Pearl Harbor, taken from *Enterprise*.

A rare photo showing the *Enterprise* and *Lexington* (in the background) operating together for the first and only time, during the Wake expedition. The destroyer *Flusser* is alongside *Enterprise*.

The first US carrier raids

Given the overwhelming superiority of the Japanese, the only feasible tactic seemed to be hit-and-run raids. Illustrated here are Halsey's strikes, against the Marshalls in early February and against Wake and Marcus later that month. Neither did much damage but were useful for gaining experience, and were much-needed morale-boosters.

come back to haunt all the Allies, especially in the comment made by the British Admiral Sir William James, after the defeat of the ABDA fleet in the Java Sea: "Once we had to choose between guns and butter—we chose butter, but our enemies chose guns. Today, we have to choose between ships and the shipwreck of everything we love."

In the early months of 1942, the combined Far East forces of American, British, Dutch and Australian (ABDA) ships amounted to only 2 heavy cruisers, 7 light cruisers, 23 destroyers and 46 submarines. Half of the destroyers and the subs were American, and armed with very poor torpedoes. Their adversary, the Japanese Southwest Pacific Force, was composed of 2 battleships, 3 carriers, 14 heavy cruisers, 5 light cruisers, 43 destroyers and an undetermined number of submarines. All of these vessels were armed with the world's finest torpedo.

Everywhere the Allies looked, they were outnumbered. With very limited options available, the priority was given to the defense of Australia and the lines of supply to that continent. Pearl Harbor was the key link in this defense. Unable to destroy the US Fleet away from Pearl, Japan decided to strike at the base's northern perimeter with an overwhelming fleet which would force Nimitz to commit everything that he had.

Seven months after the beginning of the Pacific war, the Battle of Midway should have been Japan's most complete victory. Instead, her Navy was stopped and decisively defeated. There was a certain amount of luck and a lot of skill on the American side, versus Japanese over-confidence and poor disposition of their vastly superior fleet (some groups were separated by hundreds of miles and could not support each other). Admiral Yamamoto's diversionary strike at the Aleutians was intended to pull the US carriers up north while his main force occupied Midway. The feint did not fool anyone. It is difficult to understand why Yamamoto did not immediately bring his Northern Area Force—which included 2 aircraft carriers with over 60 aircraft—down to Midway as extra insurance. Did over-confidence also influence this decision? After all, his Midway strike and support forces amounted to 11 battleships, 6 aircraft carriers, 19 cruisers, 68 destroyers, 18 submarines and over 300 aircraft. Meanwhile, his opponents could muster only 3 carriers, 8 cruisers, 17 destroyers and 233 aircraft. Yamamoto should have been able to force Nimitz to play his game, yet this was not the case. Rear Admiral Spruance masterfully kept his carriers far enough away to prevent Yamamoto from rushing in with his battleships and catching the defenseless American ships in a night surface engagement. This negated most of Yamamoto's superiority in ships and firepower.

The photographs in this chapter cover the first 7 months of the war. There were not very many pictures taken during this period. Many of the photos which were available were printed almost immediately time and again and in an effort to build morale. This was especially true of the Doolittle Raid against Tokyo and the Battles of Coral Sea and Midway. For this reason, our photographic coverage of those three actions is relatively light.

The Marshalls strike

The destroyer *Dunlap* crosses *Enterprise*'s wake as VADM Halsey's flagship heads towards the Marshall Islands on 31 January 1942. This classic 'hit and run' strike, was the US Navy's first offensive operation against Japanese territory. It also enabled *Enterprise*'s air crews to gain valuable combat experience without excessive risks.

Another photograph taken from the *Enterprise* while en route to the Marshalls with two of her escorts, the *Northampton* and *Chester* (background). While the carrier's aircraft hit seven atolls, including Makiu in the Gilberts, both of these heavy cruisers moved close in and bombarded Wotje and Tara.

Raids on Wake and Marcus

On the same day that the British fortress of Singapore fell to the Japanese, Halsey took the *Enterprise* group out of Pearl to hit Wake Island. The Douglas SBD Dauntlesses, warming up on the *Enterprise*'s flight deck, were excellent dive-bombers. In a few months these planes would become immortal. The major drawbacks of the Dauntless were slow speed and the fact that its wings did not fold. All other US Navy carrier aircraft (except for early F4F Wildcats) were designed with folding wings to enable a greater number to be stowed.

Immediately after Wake was bombed, Halsey turned the task force north, towards Marcus Island for another 'hit and run'. The final high speed run at the island was made by only the *Enterprise* and the cruisers *Northampton* and *Salt Lake City*. During this same period, the ABDA Fleet was being decimated by superior enemy forces in the 7-hour running gun and torpedo duel known as the Battle of Java Sea.

Hornet at sea

The *Hornet*, loaded with 15 US Army B-25 bombers, plows through heavy seas preparing to launch the first strike against the Japanese mainland. Taken on 18 April 1942.

Another view of *Hornet* in rough weather with the heavy cruiser *Vincennes*. Both ships were transferred from the Atlantic specifically for the Doolittle Raid on Japan. While damage to the enemy was minimal, it was a terrific boost to the morale of the American people. The announcement of the bombing had closely followed the loss of Bataan.

The Doolittle raid

The most spectacular of the early raids was the attack on Tokyo in April 1942 by Army B-25 medium bombers flown from the carrier *Hornet*. The raid caused little damage but great consternation among both the Japanese and American publics, who could not understand how the attack had been mounted. Flying from well outside the range of naval aircraft, the large B-25s could not land back on the carrier, but had to fly on to airfields in China after the bombing run. President Roosevelt increased the mystification by claiming that they had flown from 'Shangri-La'.

Covering force

1 The destroyer *Fanning* passes the *Enterprise* during the Doolittle operation. Almost completely hidden by the 'Big E' is the oiler *Sabine*. The *Enterprise*'s task was to provide air cover for the entire force since none of *Hornet*'s aircraft could be launched while the B-25s were parked on the flight deck. The final run was made by only the carriers and cruisers. Because of detection, the bombers had to be flown off 150 miles further out than had been planned.

2 The light cruiser *Nashville* being refueled by the oiler *Cimarron*. Both ships had also been transferred from the Atlantic with the *Hornet*, *Vincennes* and 4 destroyers.

The task force quickly reversed course after all the Doolittle Raiders got off without a mishap. Because they had been spotted, it could be expected that the ships would soon be attacked. Both of the oilers, *Sabine* (foreground) and *Cimarron* are shown off *Hornet*'s port side. The carrier's air group has been brought up to the flight deck in anticipation of trouble.

The battle of the Coral Sea

Japanese expansion continued in the Spring of 1942 with an advance to take Tulagi in the Solomons and Port Moresby in New Guinea. They were opposed by TF-17, built around the carriers *Yorktown* and *Lexington*, and a confused and drawn-out battle developed between 3 and 8 May. In the first round the Japanese light carrier *Shoho* was sunk—in exchange for a US destroyer and oiler—but on the 8th a big air battle left *Shokaku*, *Yorktown* and *Lexington* damaged. Despite the eventual loss of the *Lexington* the first carrier-versus-carrier battle was a strategic victory for the US Navy, and the first time a Japanese offensive had been checked.

Opening moves

While the *Hornet* and *Enterprise* were up north launching Doolittle's planes, TF-17 with the *Yorktown* and *Lexington* were heading south towards the Coral Sea. There are very few pictures which have survived of either the 'Waltzing Matilda' or 'Lady Lex'. This one shows the new 20mm AA mounts installed on *Yorktown* just before she left Pearl Harbor. Task Force 17 included 23 ships. In the Coral Sea, the Japanese would have 70 ships.

'Scratch one flattop!'

One of a series of spectacular photographs taken by *Yorktown* aircraft of the sinking of the Japanese light carrier *Shoho* during the Battle of Coral Sea, 7 May 1942. The *Shoho* was the first Japanese ship which the American people saw 'catching hell' from the US Navy. Her sinking—by 13 bombs and 7 torpedoes with the loss of only 3 US planes—was announced by the signal "Scratch one Flattop!" The loss of this carrier convinced the Japanese to call off the invasion of Port Moresby on New Guinea. Had Moresby fallen into enemy hands, Australia would have found itself with a dagger at its throat.

Loss of the *Lexington*

1

The relief force

Task Force 16 in the Coral Sea on 13 May 1942. This view was taken onboard the *Enterprise* looking at the *Hornet* and a *Benson* class destroyer. All of the ships which had been rushed from the Atlantic were still in dapple camouflage patterns while Pacific ships tended to be overall dark Navy Blue.

Looking at some of TF-16's escort, it is easy to spot another Atlantic Fleet ship, the heavy cruiser *Vincennes* (in dapple camouflage). The other two heavies in the background are the *Salt Lake City* and the *Louisville* or *Chester*. The destroyer in the foreground is the *Benham*. The *Vincennes* has less than three months to live, while the *Benham* would be lost in the coming November. The photograph was also taken in the Coral Sea by the *Enterprise* on 13 May.

1 Coral Sea should have been a major Allied victory—Port Moresby had been saved, the *Shoho* sunk, the large carrier *Shokaku* damaged and most of her aircraft destroyed. Her sister-ship *Zuikaku* also had her air group decimated. On the American side, only an oiler and destroyer had been sunk, and carriers *Yorktown* and *Lexington* damaged. With the *Hornet* and *Enterprise* on the way to relieve them, the 2 damaged carriers headed for Pearl and repairs. However, inexperience in damage control led to a series of internal explosions on the 'Lady Lex' and she had to be abandoned. This unique photo shows the *Yorktown* passing in the background as the *Lexington* burns.

Midway—the turning

4 June 1942.

While the Coral Sea battle was underway, the Japanese were planning the invasion of Midway. Because of codebreaking successes these plans were known to the Americans, and Pearl Harbor performed a miracle in getting the badly damaged *Yorktown* to sea to join *Enterprise* and *Hornet*. Although outnumbered, the US Navy struck first, destroying the carriers *Kaga*, *Akagi* and *Soryu*, all veterans of the Pearl Harbor attack. The fourth carrier, *Hiryu*, was also to be sunk but not before her aircraft had torpedoed the *Yorktown*. What should have been an overwhelming Japanese success turned into a massive defeat, and the turning point of the war in the Pacific.

1

2

3

4

5

point

6

7

8

Pearl performs a miracle

1 The *Yorktown* returns to Pearl after the Battle of Coral Sea on 27 May 1942. Admiral Nimitz knew that the attack on Midway was coming so he rushed repairs which would normally take 3 months. The 'Waltzing Matilda' departed Pearl on 31 May, after only 4 days. Her 50 surviving aircraft were added to by using parts of 3 other air squadrons. The *Enterprise* and *Hornet* were already back at sea. Note the mainmast of the sunken *Arizona* at *Yorktown*'s stern.

Enterprise in action

2 This rather indistinct picture is unusual in that it was captioned as *Yorktown* during the Battle of Midway on 4 June 1942. Actually, it is *Enterprise*—compare the forward part of both islands in this and the previous pictures. (The *Yorktown* has a prominent walk-around.) Very few pictures were taken of either *Enterprise* or *Hornet* during the battle, in which TF-16 was commanded by RADM Spruance because of Halsey's illness.

Yorktown is hit

3 Only the *Hiryu* temporarily escaped the fate of the sinking *Akagi*, *Kaga* and *Soryu*. This lone Japanese carrier then launched 18 dive-bombers and 6 fighters against the *Yorktown*. The few bombers which got through were incredibly accurate. Of 3 direct hits, the second was the most damaging. The bomb penetrated the smoke stack up-takes, disabled two boilers and finally caused the carrier to stop. *Yorktown* is shown after the attack is over, with smoke belching out of her funnel. Two *Sims* class destroyers are circling her as a screen.

4 Taken from the heavy cruiser *Astoria*: *Yorktown* is at work getting the fire under control and repairing damage. Engineering was able to get the carrier underway again, in time to prepare for a second strike of 10 torpedo-bombers and 6 fighters.

The second attack

5 We believe that this picture is also miscaptioned for it identifies this action as the first atttack against *Yorktown*. The three attacking planes all appear to be Kate torpedo-bombers. There were no Kates in the first attack, only high flying Val dive-bombers with fixed wheels. The Kates were part of the second attack.

6 The destroyer *Benham* alongside an unidentified cruiser. The *Yorktown* is in the background, dead in the water with a 26 degree list. Only half of the Kates survived the AA barrage. But of those 5, 4 planes were able to drop their torpedoes off both sides of the carrier simultaneously. Two torpedoes hit the *Yorktown*, both on the port side.

7 Close-up of the *Yorktown*, prematurely abandoned. Note the catwalk bent upward on the port side amidship. This is where one of the torpedoes had hit, 15 feet below the waterline. When it was obvious that she was not going down, the *Yorktown* was boarded and taken under tow. It looked as though she would make it back to Pearl. This picture was the US Navy's earliest combat use of 35mm cameras.

By now, all 4 of Nagumo's Striking Force carriers and a heavy cruiser had been sunk. This was Japan's first major defeat and marked the end of their offensive in the Pacific.

8 Another 35mm picture, a *Sims* class destroyer and a *New Orleans* class heavy cruiser pass the spot where the *Yorktown* and *Hammann* went down. All that remains is the debris in the foreground. A Japanese submarine had spotted the carrier under tow and put 3 torpedoes into her and the *Hammann* which was alongside to provide power for the carrier's pumps.

43

3. Test of strength
The Solomons Campaign, Summer 1942-Autumn 1943

Units of the Pacific Fleet exercise off the Hawaiian Islands during July 1942, in preparation for the invasion of Guadalcanal and Tulagi Islands in the Solomons chain. The heavy cruisers in the foreground are *Astoria*, *Vincennes*, *Quincy* and *New Orleans*. In the background, a *Porter* class leader (possibly the *Selfridge*) leads 5 *Farragut* class destroyers. The *Astoria*, *Vincennes* and *Quincy* would soon be on the bottom of Iron Bottom Sound, between Savo Island and Guadalcanal.

It is generally agreed that the Battle of Midway was the turning point in the Pacific since it marked the end of significant Japanese advances. However, immediately following the battle, few people on either side believed that the Japanese were anywhere close to being beaten. The Japanese Navy was very well trained and eager to prove its superiority in a prolonged clash of arms and a supreme test of will.

The clash came in the South Pacific beginning in the summer of 1942. The US Marine invasion made Guadalcanal the bleeding ground over which the test of strength took place. Control of the seas shifted on a regular basis, with the Americans able to dominate the surrounding waters during the daylight hours, only to turn them over to the 'Masters of Night Fighting' once the sun went down. The much vaunted 'Tokyo Express' would sail down 'The Slot', shoot up everything in sight, and then race back north, to get out of US aircraft range before dawn. While the Japanese never seriously contested American daylight dominance, the US Navy refused to give way to Japanese superiority in night battle tactics. This resulted in a series of bloody night engagements which would initially prove disastrous to the Allies. Eventually the US was able to develop tactics which would turn the tide against the 'Tokyo Express'.

The South Pacific continued to be the main focus of the war throughout 1943, until the initiation of the Central Pacific sweep in November. Losses were heavy on both sides, caused by a seemingly endless chain of naval battles. Despite this, Allied strength continued to grow, spearheaded by the arrival of newly built American ships. Even though the Japanese were beaten regularly, they showed no signs of weakening. However, many of their best pilots and sailors died in the South Pacific, including Admiral Yamamoto. Meanwhile, the Allies gained confidence and experience. Under Halsey, the US Navy was able to push the Japanese out of the South Pacific and to neutralize Rabaul, and destroyermen like Arleigh Burke and Frederick Moosbrugger were able to deny the Japanese use of the sea for bringing in reinforcements.

Fought during daylight hours, the Battle of Santa Cruz was very well photographed, as evidenced in this chapter. Almost all of the other sea engagements were fought at night and as such the photo coverage reflects only the aftermath of battle. Consequently, the pictures in this chapter are somewhat one-sided in that they show a predominance of Allied battle damage.

1 The invasion of Guadalcanal and Tulagi took place on 7 August 1942 covered by the 3 carriers from TG - 61.1. This photo was taken onboard *Enterprise* during D-Day, as a TBF Avenger flies low over the flight deck to drop a message.

Invasion of Guadalcanal

Although already in the planning stage, the first US amphibious operation of the war was sparked off by the news that the Japanese were already building an airfield on Guadalcanal. A month later, on 7 August 1942, US Marines were landing on Guadalcanal and Tulagi, the opening moves in one of the hardest-fought campaigns of modern warfare. No sooner were the troops ashore, however, than the US Navy suffered what was probably its worst defeat, in the disastrous night action off Savo Island.

2 While the carriers *Saratoga*, *Enterprise* and newly arrived *Wasp* were sent to the South Pacific as TG-61.1, Admiral Nimitz kept the *Hornet* close to Pearl Harbor. In the foreground is the heavy cruiser *Pensacola* with the *Hornet* and either the *San Diego* or *Juneau* and a *Sims* class destroyer in the background. They are shown during August 1942, off the Hawaiian Islands.

3 Off Tulagi, the anti-aircraft cruiser *San Juan* and the destroyer *Buchanan* and *Monssen* (both are in background) provide fire support for the invading Marines. Note the blinker light on *San Juan* which is sending a message to the vessel from which this picture was taken. The 500 Japanese defenders on Tulagi put up an extremely stiff resistance and actually 'fought to the last man'.

2

1

3

Savo Island Debacle

Part of the aftermath of the disastrous Battle of Savo Island, fought during the night of 8-9 August 1942. Four heavy cruisers were sunk, the American *Astoria*, *Vincennes* and *Quincy* and the Australian *Canberra*. The only cruiser to survive was the *Chicago*, shown in this close-up with part of her bow missing, from an enemy torpedo. The battle was a complete Japanese victory. Their cruisers and destroyers were able to achieve absolute surprise and successively decimate two separate groups of ships without damage to themselves. The Allied commanders handled their forces very poorly, with the *Chicago* especially at fault. Her commanding officer failed to warn the unsuspecting northern group (*Astoria*, *Vincennes* and *Quincy*) that the southern group, (*Chicago* and *Canberra*) had just been knocked out of action by an enemy force which was now heading their way.

1 On 31 August the hard-luck *Saratoga* had to return to Pearl Harbor for repairs because she had been again damaged by another submarine torpedo. The *Enterprise* was also at Pearl, having been damaged during the carrier-versus-carrier engagement of 24 August 1942, the Battle of the Eastern Solomons. The newly arrived *Hornet* and the *Wasp* were covering a Guadalcanal troop convoy on 15 September when the group was hit by Japanese submarines. The battleship *North Carolina*, destroyer *O'Brien* and aircraft carrier *Wasp* were all torpedoed. As shown in this photo, the *Wasp* was hit at the worst possible time, while her gasoline pumping system was operating. The burning carrier finally had to be abandoned with a loss of 193 men. The *Hornet* was now the only operational US carrier in the entire Pacific.

Wasp torpedoed

1

Cruz

26 October 1942.
A Japanese carrier task force supporting an offensive on Guadalcanal was intercepted by *Enterprise* and *Hornet*. An exchange of air strikes left *Shokaku*, *Zuiho* and *Hornet* badly damaged, but a last-ditch torpedo attack forced the *Hornet* to be abandoned.

First strike hits *Hornet*

2 The *Hornet* met her end on 26 October 1942 during the Japanese victory at the Battle of Santa Cruz. While the 'Sara' was still undergoing repairs, the *Enterprise* departed Pearl Harbor on 16 October and headed for the South Pacific in time to team up with the *Hornet* and slug it out with the Japanese carriers, *Zuikaku*, *Shokaku*, *Zuiho* and *Junyo*.

The *Zuiho* was knocked out with a large hole in her flight deck. Then came *Hornet*'s turn. First, she was hit by a bomb on the flight deck aft. Then a suicide plane glanced off the funnel and slammed into the flight deck; its bombs exploded and caused several fires. Two minutes later, both firerooms and the forward engine room were flooded when the carrier was hit by 2 aerial torpedoes (both on the starboard side). The ship went dead in the water. Dive-bombers then put 3 more bombs into the ship. Finally, another suicider crashed into the port forward 5in gun gallery.

A picture taken by the destroyer *Anderson* alongside the drifting *Hornet*. Meanwhile, *Hornet*'s dive-bombers hit the *Shokaku* with at least three 1,000lb bombs which wrecked her flight deck and caused fierce fires inside the hangar.

Another photo taken by *Anderson*, looking at *Hornet*'s port side. Of poor quality, the original negative was not available. Her sister-ship, the *Enterprise*, had escaped attack at this time because she had been hidden by a rain squall.

Second strike discovers *Enterprise*

While the *Enterprise* and *Hornet* strike aircraft were able to hit several Japanese ships, they failed to locate and hurt either the *Zuikaku* or *Junyo*. Once the *Enterprise* cleared the rain squall, she was attacked by enemy planes. This picture graphically captures the fury of the Battle of Santa Cruz. The twisting and turning *Enterprise* is shown smoking, probably from the second bomb hit, as 4 of her 6 escorting destroyers help fill the sky with anti-aircraft fire.

The *Enterprise*—seen from the battleship *South Dakota*—was a prime target of the attacking aircraft. Japanese dive-bombing was the most accurate in the world, as this picture graphically illustrates.

¹*South Dakota* hits back—26 planes shot down

1 A Val dive-bomber goes down in flames as a near-miss rocks the *Enterprise*. The *South Dakota*, her AA guns smoking, races along. During the second Japanese strike of 44 planes, the 'So Dak' helped to knock down 26 of them. Japanese aircraft losses during the entire battle amounted to approximately 100 aircraft. US losses totalled 74 planes including those on the *Hornet*.

Quick thinking saves the *Smith*

A Val dive-bomber flames under the *South Dakota*'s guns. The use of the medium range 40mm AA gun proved to be highly effective. It filled the gap between the 5in and the 20mm, hitting dive-bombers before they released their bombs. The Japanese Navy never filled this gap and it was to cost them dearly. A major lesson learned from the Battle of Santa Cruz was the need for a considerable increase in the number of the new 40mm guns.

A view of the kamikazied destroyer *Smith* alongside the battleship *South Dakota* on 28 October 1942. During the Japanese second air strike, a Kate torpedo-bomber crashed into the *Smith*'s No 1 gun and transformed her into a flaming torch. Smart handling and quick thinking saved the 'tin can'. The *Smith* ran into the *South Dakota*'s wake, washing off most of the burning oil and gasoline. Despite 51 casualties, the *Smith* returned to her station and used her after battery.

Third strike beaten off

Taken from the *South Dakota* as the *Enterprise* continues to be straddled by bombs. The third Japanese air strike (the second against the 'Big E') lost 24 out of 29 aircraft. The *Hornet* did not have the benefit of a battleship's AA defenses, and it is believed that the *South Dakota* made the difference and saved the *Enterprise* from her sister's fate. The carrier took only one near-miss during the third attack, but both *South Dakota* and *San Juan* each took a direct hit.

Hornet's deathblow

The heavy cruiser *Northampton* moves into position to take the helpless *Hornet* under tow, while the *Enterprise* fights off enemy aircraft just over the horizon. After several hours of towing, it appeared as though the *Hornet* would survive to fight another day. Meanwhile, Admiral Kinkaid took the *Enterprise* group south, leaving the *Hornet* group to fend for itself.

1

1 This damaged and scratched but remarkable picture shows the 'straw that broke the camel's back'. Just when it looked as though the *Hornet* might be able to raise her own steam, 9 Kate torpedo-bombers from the *Junyo* came in for the kill, forcing the *Northampton* to slip the towline. Despite fierce AA, one Kate (shown) released a torpedo which hit the *Hornet* on the starboard side, just under the island. The un-flooded after engine room was ripped open and the carrier took an 18 degree list to starboard. She was abandoned and the destroyers *Mustin* and *Anderson* tried to finish her off with 9 torpedoes but she refused to sink. They then poured 400 rounds of 5in shells in her. The *Hornet* was ablaze from stem to stern. This light beacon attracted a Japanese surface force, and the US destroyers hastily retreated. Four enemy torpedoes finally sent her to the bottom and the Battle of Santa Cruz was over.

Black Friday

13 November 1942.

This night's 'Tokyo Express' was increased to include 2 battleships, and the resulting actions with the US cruiser/destroyer force was one of the most desperate of the war. The US Navy lost 2 light cruisers and 4 destroyers, with serious damage to the cruisers *Portland* and *San Francisco*, while the Japanese lost 2 destroyers. However, the following morning the damaged battleship *Hiei* was sunk by US aircraft, the cruiser *Kinugasa* was sent to the bottom that evening, and the battle was concluded on the night of 15 November, with the destruction of the battleship *Kirishima* by shellfire from the *Washington*.

The heavy cruiser *San Francisco* limps back into Pearl Harbor. During the night of 13 November 1942 ('Black Friday') she lead a US force of 2 heavy cruisers, 3 light cruisers and 8 destroyers into Iron Bottom Sound (that body of water between Guadalcanal and Savo Island). Admiral Callaghan with his flag in *San Francisco*, was ordered to stop the 'Tokyo Express' from bombarding Henderson Airfield and the Marines ashore. Admiral Abe came down 'The Slot' with a vastly superior force of 2 battleships, 1 light cruiser and 11 destroyers. The damaged, but usable *Enterprise*, left Noumea on 11 November, as did the battleships *Washington* and *South Dakota*. However, they arrived too late to help the out-gunned cruisers.

San Francisco's damage

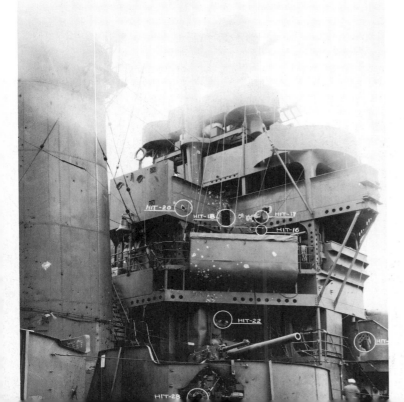

The beached *Kyushu Maru*

One of 11 Japanese troop transports which sailed down 'The Slot' under almost constant air attack. Six were sunk; a seventh, badly damaged, returned to Shortland. 14 November had been a disastrous day for the Japanese. The 4 remaining transports were beached at Tassafaronga, Guadalcanal, in an attempt to land troops during the night. The next day, the 'Cactus Air Force' from Henderson wrecked them before they could unload any equipment although their troops did get ashore.

Close-up of the back of *San Francisco*'s bridge, holed and splintered during the first stage of a nearly continuous 3-day naval engagement known as the Battle of Guadalcanal. Admiral Callaghan, Captain Young and almost all of the bridge personnel were killed during the early morning hours of 13 November. The *San Francisco* received over 40 hits, but none did any serious structural or machinery damage.

When daylight arrived on the morning of 13 November, Iron Bottom Sound was filled with the dead and wounded ships of both sides. Those Japanese ships which could get away did so, for daylight meant that American planes would control the skies. The Japanese battleship *Hiei*, unable to escape, was sunk during the day by aircraft from Henderson and the approaching *Enterprise*. The destroyer *Yudachi*, was blown up by shellfire from the damaged *Portland*. The anti-aircraft cruiser *Atlanta*, finally had to be abandoned and scuttled. Her sister-ship, *Juneau*, was torpedoed by a submarine after the battle and blew up killing almost her entire crew, including the 5 Sullivan brothers. Four US destroyers also went down, 2 during the night and the other 2 during the day.

Victor in a gunnery duel

The hero of the last phase of the Battle of Guadalcanal, the battleship *Washington*. During the night of 14-15 November the *Washington*, *South Dakota* and 4 destroyers engaged a 'Tokyo Express' which included 1 battleship, 2 heavy cruisers, 2 light cruisers and 9 destroyers. The US destroyers and the *South Dakota* were all knocked out of action, but Admiral Lee fought his flagship magnificently and sank the battleship *Kirishima*. This ended the battle and kept the Japanese from attempting any more significant attempts to bombard US positions or interfere with supply lines. The 'Tokyo Express' now went on the defensive and under the able leadership of Admiral Tanaka, did its best to supply the Imperial forces on Guadalcanal.

1

Tassafaronga

30 November 1942.
Despite increasing US Navy successes in night actions, the Japanese won a resounding victory at Tassafaronga when a large force of US cruisers and destroyers was routed by 8 Japanese destroyers. USS *Northampton* was sunk and 3 other cruisers heavily damaged in return for 1 Japanese destroyer sunk.

2

3

4

5

included the heavy cruisers *Minneapolis* (flagship), *New Orleans*, *Pensacola* and *Northampton*, the light cruiser *Honolulu* and 6 destroyers.

Despite a lack of training, Wright's force entered Iron Bottom Sound on the night of 30 November 1942 with the purpose of intercepting Tanaka's supply and reinforcement group of 8 destroyers. While the Japanese had no radar, TF-67 did.

Bringing home the survivors

2 The Battle of Tassafaronga was an absolute Japanese victory, as evidenced by the photograph of a PT boat entering Tulagi with its decks full of survivors from the sunken *Northampton*. The damaged *New Orleans* is in the background, with the destroyer *Maury* alongside.

3 The *Pensacola* still under repairs on 17 December 1942. Note the large hole directly below her short tripod mainmast. The torpedo hole is in the process of being temporarily plated over. The *Pensacola* was the third cruiser in the line and the third cruiser to be hit by a spread of torpedoes fired by Tanaka's retreating destroyers.

Initially, the Japanese were surprised by an undetected broadside of 20 torpedoes fired from 4 of Wright's destroyers concealed in the darkness. Incredibly, all 20 were either defective, or missed! The *Honolulu*, the fourth in the line, was able to dodge everything that came her way. Last in line, the *Northampton* took 2 torpedoes which would turn her into an enormous torch and result in her loss. Tanaka lost only 1 destroyer.

New Orleans' bow blown off

4 A close-up of the forward portion of the *New Orleans* at Tulagi. When the flagship, immediately in front of *New Orleans*, was hit by 2 torpedoes, the 'No Boat' sheered off to avoid collision and was caught by another torpedo. The forward magazines detonated and blew off the bow. While the US destroyers at the Battle of Tassafaronga used radar and missed, the Japanese were able to locate and fire at the US cruisers because once they opened fire, they would light up like Christmas trees in the night. The US Navy lacked flashless powder.

Another victim of the 'Long Lance'

1 The heavy cruisers *New Orleans* (CA-32) and *Minneapolis* at Espiritu Santo during the end of November. They were part of a special anti-'Tokyo Express' force which was designed to catch and kill Tanaka's destroyers as they came down 'The Slot'. Under the command of Admiral Wright, TF-67

5 The battle-damaged *Minneapolis* in drydock at Pearl Harbour for repairs during March 1943. Her bow had been blown off and a hole ripped into her port side (hidden by scaffolding) by 2 hits from 'Long Lance' torpedoes during the Battle of Tassafaronga.

The other side of the coin

One of the 12 Japanese destroyers which was lost during the struggle for Guadalcanal. This unidentified vessel was one of the numerous derelicts which dotted the beaches of Florida Island. The US Navy had lost a total of 14 destroyers in the Guadalcanal Campaign, and Admiral Nimitz acknowledged that Japanese destroyers and their crews were superior in skill, especially during torpedo attacks.

Noumea and Espiritu Santo

The greatest distances between areas of the Pacific campaigns implied the use of forward bases. While warfare was concentrated around the Solomon Islands, the US Navy used the anchorages at Noumea in New Caledonia, and Espiritu Santo in the New Hebrides. Both were to the south and east of the battle area and relatively safe.

1 Onboard the *Enterprise* on 17 December 1942. After taking part in the Battle of Guadalcanal in a damaged condition, the carrier returned to Noumea where makeshift repairs were completed on 4 December 1942. The following day was highlighted by the arrival of the newly repaired *Saratoga* at Noumea. The *Enterprise* then moved to Espiritu Santo.

2 HMNZS *Achilles* maintains station just ten minutes after a Japanese dive-bomber put a bomb on top of her No 3 turret and knocked it out of action. Crewmen are on the turret's roof inspecting damage. The *Achilles* was a unit of RADM Tisdale's distant support group which was covering RADM Ainsworth's bombardment of Munda airfield, New Georgia on 6 January 1943.

Allied reinforcements

3 Free French destroyer *Le Triomphant* at Espiritu Santo as seen from the USS *Fletcher* on 4 May 1943. The super destroyer is wearing a unique camouflage pattern which is rather difficult to see because the ship is nearly in silhouette. During this same period, American and Australian warships were painted one overall color, either Navy Blue or Dark Gray.

HMS *Victorious* rests at anchor in the Great Road at Noumea on 21 May 1943. The British carrier had arrived 4 days earlier as the replacement for *Enterprise* which was beginning a much needed overhaul. *Victorious'* aircraft had been replaced with American planes. She spent the summer in the South Pacific operating with the *Saratoga* as part of TF-14. When the *Victorious* returned to Pearl on 12 August 1943, her replacement was waiting for her: the *Essex* was the first of the war-built fleet carriers to join the Pacific Fleet.

Kula Gulf and Kolombangara

Night battles continued to be a feature of the Solomons campaign. On the night of 5-6 July 1943 the cruiser *Helena* was sunk while TG-36.1 was in action with 10 Japanese destroyers in Kula Gulf, and on 13 July the same Task Group sank the cruiser *Jintsu* at Kolombangara, although 3 Allied cruisers were heavily damaged. The Japanese never forgot the art of night-fighting.

The Battle of Kula Gulf

The light cruisers *Helena*, *St Louis* and *Honolulu* out of Tulagi, on 20 June 1943. They formed the cruiser component of Admiral Ainsworth's TG-36.1, with 4 destroyers. On 6 July, they joined battle with 10 enemy destroyers coming down Kula Gulf to reinforce Vila-Stanmore on Kolombangara. As usual, it was a ferocious night battle with the Japanese destroyers firing salvoes of the enormous 24in 'Long Lance' torpedo. The result was the loss of the *Helena*. She was successively hit by 3 torpedoes which blew away the cruiser's midships.

The wrecked Japanese *Nagatsuki* at Kolombangara Island. As one of the 10 destroyers to take part in the Battle of Kula Gulf, she had run aground trying to dodge US ships, when the vessel became a target for aircraft. The *Nizuki* was also sunk and 5 other Japanese destroyers were damaged.

The Battle of Kolombangara

HMNZS *Leander* was assigned to replace the lost *Helena* in Ainsworth's TG-36.1. The picture was taken at Tulagi, just before the task group went into action during the early morning hours of 13 July 1943. The Battle of Kolombangara took place at nearly the same location as the earlier Battle of Kula Gulf. The Japanese came down with 1 light cruiser and 5 destroyers. The Allies came up 'The Slot' with 3 light cruisers and 10 destroyers.

The Japanese got off the first torpedo salvo and one of them hit the *Leander*. Seriously damaged, she made it back to Tulagi where temporary repairs were undertaken. Twenty-eight of her crew were killed. The Japanese flagship was the cruiser *Jintsu*, which became the focal point for American shells and torpedoes—she broke in two, exploded and sank.

The *Leander* is shown at Tulagi on 25 July after the battle, low by the bow and undergoing repairs. A US sub is passing between *Leander* and the destroyer *Nicholas* which took this picture.

More 'Long Lance' victims

As the Japanese destroyers retired, they fired a salvo of torpedoes from tubes which had been reloaded in the half hour since they had first hit the *Leander*. The *St Louis* took one in the bow, as witnessed by the close-up of the damaged ship back at Tulagi.

Next hit was the *Honolulu*. One torpedo took off her bow, and a dud also bounced against her stern. This view shows the *Honolulu* at Tulagi with the repair ship *Medusa* alongside. The damaged *St Louis* is in the background. While 3 cruisers were damaged by Japanese torpedoes, only 1 destroyer (*Gwin*) was sunk. However, 2 more were damaged

From the Nicholas

The *Fletcher* class destroyer *Nicholas* which took part in the battle of Kula Gulf, was the flagship of DESRON 21 (Destroyer Squadron 21), under the command of Captain McInerney. As flagship she was assigned a photographer's mate who was responsible for the following views taken during the Central Solomons campaign.

HMAS *Warramunga* comes up to the destroyer *Nicholas* during July 1943.

in a collision following the confusion of the unexpected second torpedo attack. The lesson of Admiral Ainsworth's observation was well taken: "Looking over one's shoulder, one can always see how we should have done differently, and no one knows the fallacy of chasing Jap destroyers with cruisers better than I."

1 Taken by *Nicholas*, this panorama shows four *Fletcher* class destroyers at Purvis Bay, Florida Island during August 1943. The *Pringle*, in the foreground, was in a number of successful actions against enemy destroyers, aircraft and troop barges. She would meet her end at the hands of a kamikaze off Okinawa.

2 Close-up of the *Warramunga* alongside the *Nicholas*. The *Warramunga* was one of three improved 'Tribal' class destroyers built in Australia.

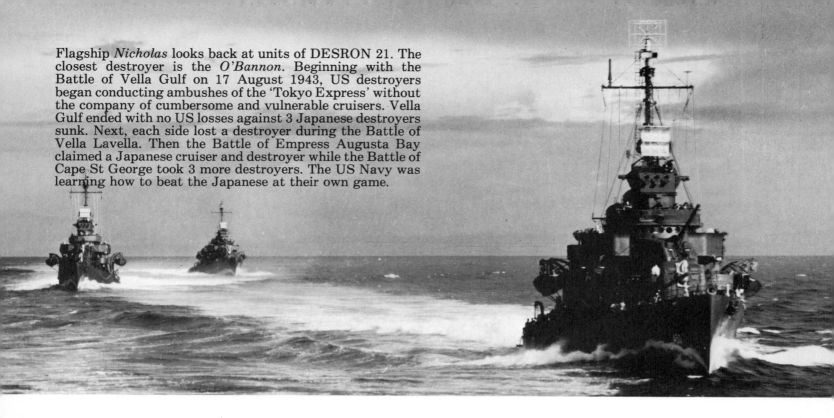

Flagship *Nicholas* looks back at units of DESRON 21. The closest destroyer is the *O'Bannon*. Beginning with the Battle of Vella Gulf on 17 August 1943, US destroyers began conducting ambushes of the 'Tokyo Express' without the company of cumbersome and vulnerable cruisers. Vella Gulf ended with no US losses against 3 Japanese destroyers sunk. Next, each side lost a destroyer during the Battle of Vella Lavella. Then the Battle of Empress Augusta Bay claimed a Japanese cruiser and destroyer while the Battle of Cape St George took 3 more destroyers. The US Navy was learning how to beat the Japanese at their own game.

On the offensive

The withdrawal from Guadalcanal in February 1943 marked the first Japanese retreat. Thereafter the US went on to the offensive, beginning in June with an attack on Munda in New Georgia, followed by landings on Vella Lavella in August and Bougainville in October. Meanwhile, in New Guinea the Japanese lost Nassau Bay in June, and on 26 December the Allies landed at Cape Gloucester on New Britain.

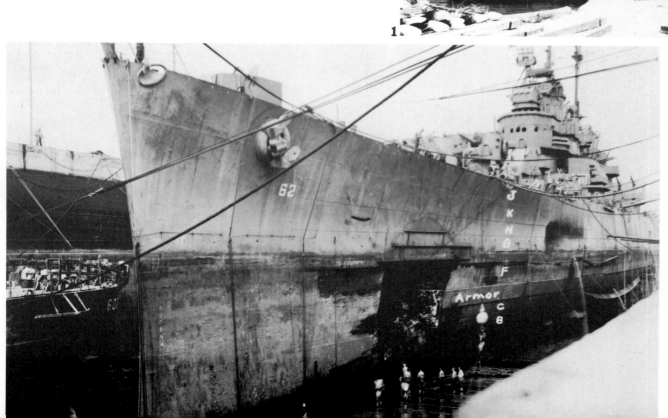

Navy repair facilities

1 The PT base at Rendova set up after the success of the New Georgia campaign, with two boats in floating drydocks. The American supply, repair and maintenance capabilities were outstanding, thus allowing these little boats to get rapidly back into action.

2 The light cruiser *Birmingham* in drydock after receiving bomb and torpedo damage while fighting off Japanese aircraft in Empress Augusta Bay on 4 November 1943, following the successful landings on Bougainville. Note the large hole in *Birmingham*'s port bow. *Birmingham*'s gunners shot down the plane which torpedoed their ship. Nine of the 30 attacking planes were shot down by a force which included the light cruisers *Santa Fe*, *Birmingham*, *Mobile* and 4 destroyers.

Invasion of New Britain

3 The 15-gun cruiser *Nashville* fires at Cape Gloucester, New Britain during the early morning hours of 26 December 1943. The radar directed gunfire used the wrecked destroyer *Mikazuki* as a beacon to cover the initial landings made by the US Marines

4 Marines and Coast Guardmen push a jeep ashore at Cape Gloucester on 26 December. This invasion was spearheaded by General MacArthur's Southwest Pacific Forces. Instead of going after Rabaul on the eastern tip of New Britain, Cape Gloucester at the extreme opposite end, was taken. This was part of the process known as 'leap frogging'—a strong enemy fortress, like Rabaul, would be completely ignored by landing behind it, and thus cutting off its supply and escape routes.

Hollandia landings

5 Hollandia, New Guinea, was successfully invaded on 22 April, 1944. This amphibious invasion was another 'leap-frog' move which by-passed Japanese strong points and enabled the landing to proceed virtually unopposed. Shown are *LST-464*, *LST-465* and *LST-454* unloading at Humbolt Bay.

Salute to the victims of Iron Bottom Sound

6 The 5 destroyers of DESRON 12 (Destroyer Squadron 12) salute 3 of their squadron mates which rest on the bottom of Iron Bottom Sound. The squadron, as photographed on 1 April 1944, has just returned from a successful foray against Rabaul. The ominous-looking island in the background is Savo Island.

During the Battle of Cape Esperance (October 1942) DESRON 12 lost the *Duncan*, which went down west of Savo. Then during the first stage of the Battle of Guadalcanal (November 1942), both the *Barton* and *Monssen* were sunk. They lie just underneath their 3 squadron mates on the left.

4. Counter Attacks
The Central Pacific, Summer 1943-Spring 1944

Symbolic of the US Navy's growing power, a squadron of SB2C Helldivers from the carrier *Bunker Hill* on their way to hit the Japanese fortress of Truk in the Carolines (17 February 1944). This was the US Navy's most daring attack to date.

The middle of 1943 through 1944 saw a major expansion of the US Pacific Fleet, and the American Navy began to flex its new muscles. Of special significance was the combat debut of Grumman's F6F Hellcat fighters and the large *Essex* class aircraft carriers. As the foundation of the new and all powerful Fast Carrier Task Force, the Hellcats and *Essex*es would soon become the key players in the Battle for the Pacific. By the end of the war, the F6F had achieved an incredible 19:1 kill ratio—Hellcat pilots shot down 19 enemy planes for every one of their own lost to opposing aircraft.

At the start of 1943, the US Navy had only 2 fast carriers still afloat in the entire Pacific. One of these, the *Enterprise*, was in need of both repair and overhaul. Just one year later, there were 14 fast carriers in the Pacific, with 5 'working up' in the Atlantic and 10 more under construction on the East Coast. Out of a total of 29 fast carriers in the US Navy's 1944 inventory, 18 were *Essex*es, while 9 were of the smaller *Independence* class, converted from light cruisers. All of the *Independence*s, and 14 of the *Essex*es would see combat before the war was over.

By comparison, Japan's equivalent fast carrier force totalled 9 semi-operational vessels with 6 more being built. Only one of the carriers under construction would ever operate aircraft against the US Navy.

The *Essex* class were superb ships, ideally suited for Pacific operations. Capable of carrying 100 aircraft (the *Independence*s would handle only 35 planes each), they soon became the principal targets of the entire Japanese Navy and Air Force. Despite this, none of the *Essex*es were lost to enemy action. This was due to a combination of the magnificent efforts of their crews and outstanding damage control provisions built into each carrier.

This period also introduced the rest of the winning team—those ships and aircraft which balanced out the Fast Carrier Strike Force. The pictures in this chapter vividly portray the entire team and their growing numbers. With the vastness of the Pacific as a backdrop, the reader is able to view the growing power of the United States 'on the move'.

Operations in the Central Pacific were noticeably different from the South Pacific. The camera captures this difference

as we make note of the sparsity of photographs of ships in harbor. The spotlight shifted from the South to the Central Pacific in November 1943, with the US Navy maintaining the initiative. The vast empire which Japan had conquered early in the war soon became a liability. The numerous far-flung islands proved impossible to defend adequately. These isolated outposts were ideal targets for fast carrier warfare. The mobile US Navy was able to move massive concentrations of power against remote islands, destroy the local defenses and then move on to yet another target. This was particularly beneficial to inexperienced American sailors and airmen, who were able to get actual combat training without unacceptable risks. Thus began the piecemeal destruction of Japan's outer ring of 'unsinkable aircraft carriers' (islands with airfields).

While the Fast Carrier Task Force struck from the outside, US submarines gnawed away at Japan's insides—her vital lines of supply. During this period, the Japanese Combined Fleet operated out of Truk, under the command of Admiral Koga. Spearheaded by 3 carriers and 6 battleships, this force went looking for the US Navy in September. It did not find them. The raids on Wake during October convinced Koga that it would be the next amphibious target. He was wrong. Again, he could not find the US Navy.

On 1 November, Admiral Koga made a fatal error. He stripped his only 3 operational carriers of all of their aircraft and sent them south to Rabaul. That base now held 373 aircraft for the defense of Bougainville. Without aircraft, Koga's carriers were useless. Without carriers to provide air cover for his battleships, they too dropped out of the picture. A series of air strikes from US carriers covering the invasion of Bougainville then hit Rabaul. They disabled Koga's cruisers and decimated his air groups. Of the 173 carrier aircraft on loan, only 52 returned to their carriers on 13 November. The rest had been lost. Worse still, almost half of all of his highly trained air crews were killed.

Without aircraft for his carriers, Koga dared not send out his surface ships. Therefore, the invasions of the Gilberts and Marshalls were able to proceed without interference from the Japanese Navy.

Preparing a path

Before the Central Pacific offensive began in earnest, a number of raids on outlying islands were carried out. These were useful for training the growing US carrier forces, but also served to camouflage American strategic intentions.

The US build-up

1 USS *Yorktown* heads towards Pearl Harbor during the Summer of 1943. She was the second of the new *Essex* class fleet carriers to report to the Pacific. As with all ships transiting from the mainland to Pearl, *Yorktown*'s decks were filled with vehicles and replacement aircraft.

2 The *Bunker Hill* was the fourth *Essex* to report to the Pacific. This incredible picture was taken on 29 September 1943 on top of the carrier's aftermost radio lattice mast—a very daring and dangerous feat with the vessel underway.

3 The new *Yorktown* on the way to raid Marcus Island on 1 September 1943. She was accompanied by the *Essex* and *Independence*. All 3 carriers were operating the Grumman F6F Hellcat fighter.

On 18-19 September, the *Lexington*, *Princeton* and *Belleau Wood* hit the Gilbert Islands. These raids were limited-risk operations which were invaluable training to new pilots, and made the next invasion target more difficult for the Japanese to forecast.

Diversionary raids

4 The light carrier *Belleau Wood* passes the heavy cruiser *Minneapolis* on 5 October 1943 during the raid on Wake Island. This raid was mounted by the largest US carrier task force yet to be assembled. It included the *Essex*, *Yorktown*, *Lexington*, *Independence*, *Belleau Wood* and *Cowpens*.

5 Another photograph taken onboard the *Minneapolis* on 5 October 1943. The 8in guns are being cleaned after the completion of the day's bombardment against Wake. The cruiser's new, smaller bridge is evident in this view (compared with the photo in Chapter 3). The *Minneapolis* was one of 7 cruisers and 24 destroyers which took part in the raid.

A Grumman TBF Avenger torpedo-bomber from the *Yorktown* flies over her mothership in the Central Pacific during October 1943. The single torpedo was carried internally.

Rabaul strike

The Japanese fleet under air attack at Rabaul. Several *Nachi* class heavy cruisers are getting underway. The carrier air strikes successfully damaged and neutralized the enemy fleet during raids on 6 and 11 November. Japanese carrier air groups were also stationed at Rabaul at this time and suffered accordingly. Against the loss of 28 US aircraft, 89 Japanese planes were shot down. Rabaul was thus negated as a 'force to be reckoned with' during the upcoming invasions of Bougainville in the South and the Gilberts in the Central Pacific.

1

2

3

1 This picture was taken from the light carrier *Independence*'s flight deck, looking down at the forward-most 40mm quad mount on the forecastle. During the air strikes against Rabaul on 11 November, the *Independence* was near-missed by 4 bombs. A fifth bomb, dropping on top of the carrier, was detonated in mid-air by a 40mm round from one of the vessel's guns.

2 This picture was taken from the carrier *Lexington* looking at the oiler *Guadalupe* and the destroyer *Maury* refueling alongside. As units of the newly established Fifth Fleet, these vessels were part of an armada which now included 11 carriers, 6 battleships, 6 cruisers, 21 destroyers and 8 escort carriers.

3 An SBD dive-bomber takes off from the *Lexington* on 12 November 1943.

Invasion of the

ember 1943.
ntral Pacific offensive opened with an
ious assault on the Gilbert Islands of Tarawa
kin. Tarawa fell after a very bloody 3-day
and Makin surrendered on 24 November.

2

4

3

Gilbert Islands

5

6

Battleship fire support

1 The battleship *Maryland* lets go with a practice salvo from her main battery on 12 November. Her 16in guns would provide fire support at the upcoming invasion of Tarawa on 19-20 November.

2 Three *Colorado* men watch as the *Maryland* steams off the starboard side. The *Tennessee* is just visible over the *Maryland*'s fantail.

Carrier air support

3 Part of TF-50 off the Gilberts on 15 November 1943. The picture was taken from the *Lexington* looking at the *Cowpens* and *Yorktown* (background). The carrier task force remained off the Gilberts to protect the amphibious fleet.

4 An SBD dive-bomber catapulted from the *Lexington* at sundown off the Gilberts.

5 An SBD flies over the battleship *Washington* and the *Lexington* (in the background) off the Gilberts during November.

Logistic support

6 Two views taken from the new *Lexington* and the new *Neosho*, refueling alongside, off the Gilbert Islands. The first *Neosho* and the first *Lexington* were both lost at the Battle of Coral Sea.

Tarawa

Some of the carnage on the beaches of Tarawa, Gilbert Islands on 22 November 1943. The landing craft were not able to clear the outer reef. This forced the Marines to wade ashore in deep water and in the face of murderous enemy fire.

The Marshalls

The next target after the Gilberts was the Marshalls group, the atolls of Majuro and Eniwetok being taken in January-February 1944. Most of the Japanese opposition was encountered on Kwajalein which finally surrendered on 7 February.

The growing carrier force

Taken from the *Yorktown*, over an unidentified oiler and the cruiser *Portland*, looking at the venerable *Enterprise* (1 December 1943). On 26 November, the 'Big E' introduced carrier-based night-fighter operations in the Pacific when a 3-plane team broke up a large group of land-based bombers attacking TF-50.

On 4 December, the *Yorktown* and *Enterprise* raided Kwajalein and destroyed 65 enemy planes against 5 US losses.

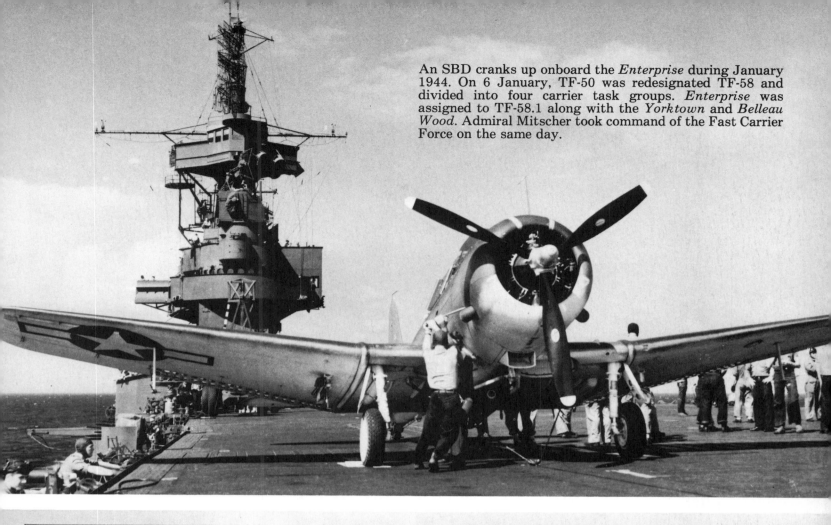

An SBD cranks up onboard the *Enterprise* during January 1944. On 6 January, TF-50 was redesignated TF-58 and divided into four carrier task groups. *Enterprise* was assigned to TF-58.1 along with the *Yorktown* and *Belleau Wood*. Admiral Mitscher took command of the Fast Carrier Force on the same day.

With the invasion fleet

The veteran destroyer *Ellet* transferring mail from the amphibious force flagship *Appalachian* while on the way to the invasion of the Marshalls. The picture was taken on 17 January 1944. The *Ellet* was in the Pacific when the war began, covered the *Enterprise* during the Doolittle Raid and fought with distinction in the South Pacific (where she sank the submarine *I-168*).

Screening force

Battleship Division 7 was composed of the brand new *Iowa* (foreground) and *New Jersey* (background). As part of TG-58.2, the upcoming campaign against the Marshalls was the first operation for both ships. The *New Jersey* had joined up on 25 January 1944. This picture was taken just before the 29 January invasion. It is easy to see how the *New Jersey* got her nickname 'The Black Dragon'.

The *Intrepid* was the fifth *Essex* to report to the fast carrier force. This picture was taken just after she joined TF-58.2 in January 1944. The *Lexington* had been damaged by an aerial torpedo a month earlier and was on the West Coast for repairs. Despite this, TF-58 was now composed of 6 large and 6 light carriers.

The battleship *South Dakota*, followed by her sister-ship *Alabama*. Both are also on their way to the Marshalls to shell Roi and Namur Islands on 1 February. After the *South Dakota* was damaged in the South Pacific, she was repaired in New York and then served with the British Home Fleet in the Atlantic. The *South Dakota*'s appearance was unique in that she was the only battleship to mount a quad 40mm AA all the way forward on her bow.

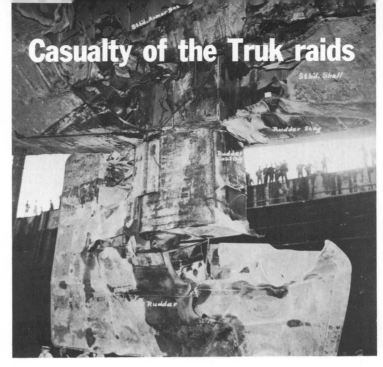

Casualty of the Truk raids

On 17 February the US Navy began a daring 3-day raid on the Japanese base at Truk, as preparation for the Eniwetok landings. The only damage to TF-58 during the raids was an aerial torpedo hit on the carrier *Intrepid*, shown here in drydock at Pearl Harbor on 26 February 1944. In terms of other damage to TF-58, a total of 25 aircraft were lost. On the other hand, the raid on Truk destroyed 125 Japanese aircraft and sank 47 ships including 1 light cruiser, 3 destroyers and a 19,000 ton tanker. This close-up clearly shows the damage to *Intrepid*'s rudder. The ship had to be steered by a make-shift 'sail' jury-rigged on the forecastle. The torpedo attack on the *Intrepid* was made at night by radar-equipped Kate torpedo-bombers. Night-fighters attempted to intercept them but were totally ineffective. During the same night, 12 of *Enterprise*'s radar-equipped TBFs scored 13 direct hits on ships at Truk, cloaked by darkness.

Returning air strike

A TBF about to 'catch the wire' onboard the *Enterprise* after a mission against Kwajalein, Marshall Islands (29 January 1944). During three days of air strikes, Mitscher's carriers destroyed the archipelago's entire air force of 150 planes. TF-58 lost 49 aircraft.

Further carrier raids

After a raid on the Marianas, *Enterprise* was detached to the South Pacific, to support MacArthur's offensive in New Guinea (March-April 1944). In the Central Pacific carrier raids struck as far west as the Palaus.

Enterprise back in action

1 Onboard the *Enterprise* en route to strike the Marianas, on 20 February 1944. The extensive suit of radar on her island reflects the benefits of her 1943 overhaul. TF-58 destroyed 168 aircraft in the Marianas as a preliminary to the upcoming invasion. Half of Japan's carrier-based aircraft were lost, disrupting the reorganization of her carrier striking fleet.

2 This beautiful picture of the *Enterprise* was taken by one of her aircraft as it raced by the carrier, yet the focus is perfectly sharp. The *Enterprise* was on her way to provide air cover and close support for the landings on Emirau Islands (19-21 March).

3 The *Enterprise* in the process of launching an air strike against Emirau in the Bismark Archipelago. The veteran carrier was part of TF-36.1 which had been detached to cover this South Pacific invasion (while the rest of TF-58 struck the Carolines) to eliminate opposition to the forth-coming US Army landing at Hollandia, New Guinea.

Emirau

Belleau Wood crewmen watch as her escorts down a Japanese bomber off Emirau.

Palau raid

Funeral services on the recently repaired *Lexington* on 3 April 1944. As part of TF-58, the carrier had just completed operations against the Palaus. Mines dropped from 3 torpedo squadrons completely blocked the main harbor, and 36 trapped Japanese ships were then sunk at leisure. Air opposition was wiped out with the destruction of 157 enemy planes, against the loss of 25 US carrier aircraft.

Saratoga in the East Indies

In March 1944 the carrier *Saratoga* and 3 destroyers were detached to join the British Eastern Fleet in the Indian Ocean. Strikes were carried out against targets in the Dutch East Indies.

East Indies

This picture was taken onboard the 'Sara' as she was led into Trincomalee Harbor, Ceylon (on 31 March 1944), following the British carrier *Illustrious*.

Allied battleships

As the 'Sara' entered the harbor, her photographer took this picture of the large Free French battleship *Richelieu*. With her speed of 32 knots, the *Richelieu* was the only battleship attached to Admiral Sir James Somerville's British Eastern Fleet which was capable of keeping up with the *Saratoga* and the *Illustrious*.

This picture was taken from the 'Sara' as she passed close to the bow of the *Valiant* on 7 April 1944. Four months later the battleship was being refitted at Trincomalee when the floating dock suddenly collapsed causing extensive damage to the ship.

A contrast in carriers

Two British carriers at Trincomalee on 10 April 1944. The *Illustrious* is in the foreground with the *Unicorn* behind her. Note all the men topside, clad only in shorts. *Illustrious* class carriers were designed as enclosed armored boxes, and as such, they were incredibly hot in tropical waters.

On 19 April Admiral Somerville led a 27-ship task force against Sabang, Sumatra, spearheaded by the *Saratoga* and the *Illustrious*.

Task force 58

As an example of the flexibility of carrier air power, a week after TF-58 supported the landings at Hollandia in New Guinea, the force mounted a major raid on Truk in the Carolines.

Aboard the *Hornet*

1 First of 4 flight deck scenes onboard the *Hornet* during April 1944. This one shows the damage to the tail surfaces of the Helldivers parked on the after end of the flight deck (caused by rough weather). *Hornet* was one of the support carriers at Hollandia, New Guinea, where 21 carrier planes were lost during the operation.

2 The evening before the second strike against Truk, *Hornet*'s anxious crewmen pace the flight deck in front of 2 Helldivers. On 29 and 30 April, TF-58 destroyed 93 Japanese planes against a total of 36 of its own aircraft lost. Most of the air crews were rescued by floatplanes and submarines (the *Tang* rescued 22 airmen off Truk).

3 A badly shot-up Helldiver, returning from a strike against Truk on 30 April, crashed and flipped over on the *Hornet*. It then caught fire. One of *Hornet*'s men is racing towards the trapped aircrew.

4 A damaged TBM Avenger from the light carrier *Cowpens* onboard the *Hornet*. The torpedo-bomber was hit over Truk on 30 April. When she landed her tail wheel collapsed because of flak damage. The belly gunner was also wounded.

After the strikes against Truk, TF-58 planes took a few swipes at Ponape and Satawan. Admiral Lee took 6 battleships close to Ponape for a bombardment run on 1 May. The task force then headed for Majuro and a rest and replenishment period in preparation for the upcoming invasion of the Marianas.

2

2

3

4

5. Showdown in the Marianas

Battle of the Philippine Sea, June 1944

Japan was determined to make a stand against further US advances in the Central Pacific. It took time to rebuild depleted carrier forces—but time was against the Japanese Navy. As each month passed, the US Navy added either a fast carrier or an escort carrier to its fleet. This was matched by growing numbers of excellent planes and trained men.

The 2½-year period from Pearl Harbor to June 1944 saw US industry complete 18 fast carriers and 60 escort carriers for their navy, plus 39 escort carriers for Great Britain! On the other hand, the combined Japanese total amounted to only 12 carriers. It had been generally understood by Japan's leaders that a successful war against America would have to be concluded in less than 2 years. After that period, the United States' tremendous industrial capability would significantly alter the outcome. Therefore, by June 1944 it was already too late for Japan—unless their navy could perform a miracle.

If their leaders held any hope of success, it was dashed by the US Navy during the Battle of the Philippine Sea. The Japanese master battle plan for the coming US invasion was faulty from the start. While it looked impressive on paper, it depended on the Americans making it convenient for the Japanese Navy, and on inflated numbers of effective land-based planes. Because of the critical shortage of tankers and refined oil, the Imperial Navy would not be able

to respond to an invasion of the too-distant Marianas, unless part of the screening fleet was left behind. This was considered unacceptable. The Marianas were exactly where the US Navy struck next. The die was cast and the decision was made to 'top off' the First Mobile Fleet directly at the oil fields with dangerously volatile crude oil. Initially, the gamble paid off. All the Japanese carriers were able to launch their strikes first. The plan then began to unravel. US submarine torpedoes sank 2 of the enemy's finest carriers (because of the crude oil). This came on top of an even greater disaster. Better than three-quarters of the aircraft in the Japanese strikes were shot down over the US Fleet, primarily by Hellcats.

The advantage of the first punch did the Japanese no good. Most of their planes were blown out of the sky without hurting the US Navy. They had taken their best shot and had nothing left. Their only consolation was that the use of crude oil had enabled them to bring along their battleships to provide a heavy anti-aircraft screen and this helped when the American planes hit them the next day—plus the fact that US pilots had flown a great distance to their targets, at the end of a long day of searches. The combination of heavy AA and exhaustion may well have prevented the massacre of the entire Japanese First Mobile Fleet. Regardless, their carrier air groups were again in shambles. They would never have enough time to recover again.

One of the most spectacular happenings of World War 2 occurred when the American planes returned to TF-58 in total darkness and very low on gas. Admiral Mitscher ordered the fleet to *turn the lights on* to guide them in. This saved the lives of hundreds of valuable men. Mitscher took a calculated risk, for if an enemy submarine had been in the vicinity, a number of 'lit up' ships could easily have been sunk, costing thousands of lives. Fortune was doubtlessly on the side of the Americans. The Marianas campaign took only 2 months.

The light cruiser *Birmingham* back with the Pacific Fleet wearing a new dazzle camouflage design (she had been damaged in the South Pacific, see Chapter 3). The battleship *Colorado* is in the background, as seen from the escort carrier *Gambier Bay* on 11 June 1944. One month later the *Colorado* was hit 22 times by shore batteries off Tinian. Four months later the *Gambier Bay* was sunk, and the *Birmingham* badly damaged, during the Battle for Leyte Gulf.

This chapter contains a mixed bag of pictures of the entire operation. Unfortunately, not-previously-reproduced photographs seem to be somewhat scarce, but the candid pictures show the US Navy almost exclusively at sea or operating off enemy-held islands. Noticeable is the relative impunity of the American ships as we make note of the fact that the most serious damage was because of a collision between two US battleships. This would change drastically in the following operations, as will be seen in later chapters.

3

4

Opening moves— Saipan 15 June 1944.

The invasion of Saipan opened the campaign against the Marianas. Following the now routine sequence of air strikes and intensive bombardment, and despite a strong Japanese counter-attack, the landings were successful.

1

2

En route for Saipan

1 USS *Evans* coming alongside to refuel on 10 June 1944. The destroyer had left Pearl Harbor on 3 June to screen the fueling and aircraft replacement group (whose function was to support both the Fast Carrier Task Force and the Carrier Escort Force during the assault on Saipan).

This picture was not chosen for its uniqueness or quality. It was selected because of the ship herself—11 months after this photograph was taken, this destroyer gained immortality off Okinawa (see Chapter 9).

2 Onboard the *Enterprise* with the Fast Carrier Task Force (TF-58) on 10 June 1944. Grumman F6F Hellcats are parked in front of the island. The design of Grumman planes were unique in that their wings folded back against the fuselage (instead of folding up, over the cockpit).

The 'Big E' left Majuro with TF-58 on 6 June. One day after this peaceful picture was taken, *Enterprise* pilots struck at Saipan, Rota, and Guam—plus supporting the landings on Saipan until 17 June.

3 A picture taken by the *Gambier Bay* on 11 June, of the *Montpelier* as she slides past on her way to commence the bombardment of Saipan on 14 June.

4 Commander Bill Martin returns to the *Enterprise* on 14 June 1944, courtesy of an escorting destroyer. His Avenger had been damaged by flak over Saipan and forced 'into the drink' where he was picked up. The US Navy policy of stationing floatplanes and submarines off the target undergoing attack (plus destroyers assigned to pick up ditched air crews) guaranteed that a high percentrage of downed aviators would be saved. This had the double advantage of returning veterans to duty and keeping morale high because the chances of being rescued were very high should anyone be shot down.

The rescued pilot in this picture went on to become the Commander of the Sixth Fleet.

Onboard the *Hornet* with the *Yorktown* framed by the forward 5in gun barrels. The picture was taken off the Marianas during June. Both carriers were part of TG-38.1 which also included the light carriers *Bataan* and *Belleau Wood*, 3 heavy cruisers, 2 AA cruisers and 14 destroyers.

Air strikes against Saipan

Helldivers from the new *Hornet* on the way to strike Saipan.

The Marianas Turkey Shoot

19 June 1944.

Having rebuilt her carrier air groups after the Rabaul disaster, Japan decided on a further attempt at the 'decisive battle' with the US Navy. However, the Japanese air crews were poorly trained and when thrown into action against TF-58 they were slaughtered in what one US airman derisively termed 'The Great Marianas Turkey Shoot'. The Japanese lost 346 airplanes, while the US lost 30.

The Japanese attack begins

Friendly aircraft fly over units of TF-58 as it maintains station off the Marianas on 16 June. The Japanese Navy was on its way and the US Navy was waiting for them. USS *New Jersey* is in silhouette in the foreground with an *Independence* class light carrier steaming in the other direction.

A wounded Hellcat pilot being helped out of his plane aboard the *Essex* during the Battle of the Philippine Sea on 19 June. The Japanese were able to hit the US Fleet first because their aircraft possessed greater range (at the expense of armor and self-sealing tanks).

Dauntless dive-bombers from *Lexington*'s VB-16 fly over the invasion fleet off Saipan on 19 June. This was the last major combat operation for the Dauntless. Most of the other carriers' bombing squadrons were already flying the big Helldiver.

Hellcats in the process of being catapulted from the *Bunker Hill* to hit the Japanese. The Hellcat fighter was the true victor of the Battle of the Philippine Sea.

Note that the carrier has only one catapult in this picture. As built, a second 'cat' was fitted in the hangar where it was relatively useless. It was removed during the *Bunker Hill*'s next refit. A second catapult was added to the flight deck, across from the existing one.

Counter-strike

A tractor full of *Yorktown* crewmen pulls a Hellcat past an Avenger torpedo-bomber. Note the vast array of antennas atop the island.

While none of America's fast carriers was even lightly damaged by the massive air strikes on 19 June, Japan lost 2 of its biggest and best, victims of 2 US subs. The only consolation was that both had already launched their planes before they were torpedoed. This substantial submarine victory was self-fulfilling since it was a direct result of the US submarine campaign against Japan's lifelines. Refined oil—and the tankers to carry it—was in such short supply that the Japanese ships were forced to use highly volatile, unrefined oil. Instead of the carriers *Taiho* and *Shokaku* simply being damaged from the torpedo hits, the unrefined oil's fumes and leaks caused massive explosions which destroyed both ships.

The day after the 'Marianas Turkey Shoot' the US Navy finally found Japan's First Mobile Fleet as it attempted to retreat out of range. At 4.21pm, on 20 June, 216 US aircraft left their carriers on one of the longest strike missions of the war. The Japanese sent up 75 aircraft as defense. When the attack was over, Japan had lost 1 aircraft carrier and 2 oilers sunk, and 3 carriers damaged. While the 216 plane strike group had left the carriers in daylight, it returned in total darkness (10.45pm). Most were nearly out of gas and had no way of finding their carriers in the darkness. In a classic example of high regard which Admiral Mitscher had for his aviators, he ordered the fleet's lights turned on. Bedlam followed as planes came down on the first deck they could find. Some planes ran out of gas and ditched alongside ships, others plowed into packed flight decks. When it was over, 116 aircraft had landed safely. The remaining 80 either ditched or crash-landed and most of the aircrews were rescued.

Crash of a flak-damaged Hellcat into *Essex*'s crash barrier. The barrier was designed to stop any plane (which had missed 'the wire') from crashing into aircraft parked forward on the flight deck. Since no tailhook is visible, it was either shot away or pulled off when it hooked the wire.

This picture was taken from the carrier *Essex* alongside a fleet oiler, looking at the destroyer *Hailey* and the carriers *Hornet* and *Enterprise* in the background. The Battle of the Philippine Sea was the greatest carrier-versus-carrier battle of all time. The Japanese lost 400 carrier planes, plus another 100 land-based aircraft. US losses totalled 130 from combat and operations.

The campaign continues

Another magnificent photograph—this time the camera captured a flight of *Yorktown* Helldivers high above their mothership. After the Marianas campaign the *Yorktown* sailed to the West Coast for a much needed refit which would cause her to miss the gigantic Battle for Leyte Gulf the following October.

The massive US victory in the Battle of the Philippine Sea sealed the fate of the Marianas, but it was a couple of weeks before Saipan was secured. Further landings were made on Guam (21 July) and Tinian (24 July) and by 12 August 1944 the Marianas were under American control.

A beautiful picture of a *Yorktown* Helldiver over TG-58.1 on 23 June 1944. The day before this picture was taken the task group's 4 carriers had sent 122 planes against Chichi and Iwo Jima. They destroyed a total of 78 Japanese planes, against 6 of their own lost.

Yorktown

1

2

3

4

5

Light cruisers

1 Two light cruisers from TF-58's screen, the *Houston* (foreground) and the *Vincennes*, executing a high speed turn on 26 June 1944. They are in the process of bombarding Guam and Rota.

Spoils of war

2 Japanese Zero fighters which were captured on Saipan, on their way to the US on 10 July 1944 aboard the escort carrier *Copahee*.

Bombardment of Guam

3 The main battery of the battleship *New Mexico* opens fire on Guam Island in the Marianas on 18 July. One of her sister-ships, the *Idaho*, is in the background.

4 A Helldiver about to ditch into 'the drink' on 19 July. The crew was rescued.

5 This great picture has no ship identification, except that it was taken on 28 July 1944, during a bombardment of Guam.

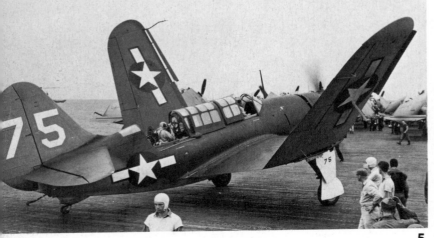

Tinian

1 Empty shell casings in the process of being stacked on the *Montpelier* on 31 July. The light cruiser has just completed bombarding Tinian which was invaded on 24 July. Tinian, the third island of the Marianas group to be assaulted, was secured on 4 August.

2 A Wildcat fighter missed both the wire and the barrier and crashed into the planes parked forward. Note the number of fire hoses standing by in case of fire. This picture was taken onboard the *Hoggatt Bay* in August.

Battleships in collision

3 Close-up of the damage to the battleship *California* after she collided with her sister-ship, the *Tennessee*. Some of the debris has already been stripped away. The repairs were made in floating drydock ABSD-1, at Espiritu Santo.

4 Repairs on the *California* were nearly completed when this picture was taken on 8 September 1944, as evidenced by the scaffoldings next to the port side bow. An anti-torpedo net is visible in the upper left of the picture.

Postscript to the Marianas campaign

5 A Helldiver in the process of folding its wings as it taxis up *Lexington*'s flight deck on 20 August 1944. TF-58 hit Palau, Yap and Ulithi during August. Once liberated, Ulithi was to become the US Navy's major forward fleet anchorage.

The Marianas operations came to a close when Guam was secured on 10 August. The Japanese lost 1,223 aircraft during the 2-month campaign.

Color Section

1. Pearl Harbor

The refloated battleship *West Virginia* alongside a pier at Pearl Harbor, about to steam for the US and a complete reconstruction. Much of the battleship's topweight has been removed, including all the secondary armament, directors, cranes and both cage masts.

1

2

3

2. Hit and run

1 The carrier *Saratoga* at Pearl Harbor. While no date has been given, the rig suggests it is in the summer of 1942, just prior to the invasion of Guadalcanal.

3. Test of strength

2 Part of the Solomons invasion fleet off Tulagi Island during August 1942. The silhouetted ships are all destroyers, except for the *Northampton* class heavy cruiser.

3 Close-up of *Enterprise*'s bomb-damaged flight deck. The picture was taken on 24 August 1942, after the Battle of the Eastern Solomons. The bomb penetrated the carrier's flight deck and exploded in the hangar, causing the flight deck to be pushed upwards. An *Atlanta* class anti-aircraft cruiser is in the background.

4 A Japanese destroyer refloated by the 34th CB (Construction Battalion), popularly known as Sea Bees, off the Halavo Seaplane Base on Florida Island.

4

1

4. Counter attacks

1 Three views of the rebuilt heavy cruiser *Minneapolis* refueling from the fleet oiler *Platte* (AO-24). The pictures were taken from the light fleet carrier *Cowpens* (CVL-25), which is refueling from the oiler's port side. Taken during November 1943, the task force was conducting raids against the Marshalls and Gilberts. The *Platte* was one of the 3 large oilers to be armed with 4-5in guns in enclosed mounts.

2 Onboard the light cruiser *Mobile* (CL-63) during the October 1943 raid against Marcus Island. The 40mm gun crew is standing by the anti-aircraft gun because of the close proximity to the Japanese held island.

3 Another photograph taken onboard the *Mobile* during the Marcus raid, looking at the carrier *Yorktown*. This view is of the cruiser's stern with the hangar hatch opened in the foreground. The observation aircraft is a Vought OS2U Kingfisher.

3

2

4

5

1 Grumman F6F-3 Hellcat fighters (folded wings) and Douglas SBD-4 Dauntless dive-bombers onboard the newly commissioned USS *Essex* (CV-9). The *Essex* was the first of the new, large and fast fleet carriers to report to the Pacific to form the highly mobile carrier task force.

2 This picture was taken from the bridge of the new battleship *Iowa*. The identity of the *Essex* class carrier in the background is uncertain, but it is believed to be the *Lexington*, taken on the East Coast of the United States.

3 The battleship *Missouri* fires her forwardmost 16in turret. The ship was still east of the canal zone at the time, probably on her 'shakedown' cruise.

4 Taken onboard an *Iowa* class battleship, possibly the *Missouri*. Note the white countershading on the undersides of the overhangs. This was intended to reduce dark shapes caused by shadows and thus reduce the ship's visibility.

5. Showdown in the Marianas

5 Taken onboard an unidentified cruiser during target practice, 'somewhere in the Pacific'. No date was given.

1 Another example of no date or ship identification, but it obviously shows a *Fletcher* class destroyer with its crew practising on a 40mm mount. The destroyer is painted in the standard Pacific camouflage scheme known as Measure 21, solid Navy Blue.

2 Taken onboard a *New Mexico* class battleship off the landing beaches at Guam during July 1944. The ship's crew is 'mustering on deck', after having taken part in the bombardment and covered the landings. The wood deck has been painted Deck Blue, although most of it has been worn off.

3 Onboard the carrier *Enterprise* (CV-6) during the spring of 1944. The center aircraft elevator is in the down position. Three Grumman TBF Avenger torpedo-bombers are on the flight deck.

7. Leyte

4 Looking at the forward twin 5in mounts onboard the USS *Intrepid* (CV-11). The photograph was miscaptioned as the *Lexington*, but her radar rig and bridge details, plus the camouflage pattern, definitely identify the vessel as the *Intrepid*, sometime between August and December of 1944.

5 Another photo captioned as USS *Lexington*, which in fact is the *Hancock* (CV-19). The Curtiss SB2C Helldivers on the flight deck are wearing the *Hancock*'s aircraft ID of the 'horseshoe'. Additionally, the two quad 40mm mounts on the fantail, and the camouflage pattern are characteristic of the *Hancock* (CV-19).

3

4

5

1 Taken from the fantail of an unidentified *Essex* class carrier as an F6F Hellcat comes in for a landing.

8. The Winter campaigns

2 The battleship *South Dakota* takes a wave over her bow as the ship operates near Okinawa on 1 March 1945. The 'So Dak's' bow-mounted quad 40mm is almost completely covered by spray.

3 Taken on the *South Dakota*'s fantail, probably at the Ulithi fleet anchorage. The after 16in turret has swung to port for the ship's band to perform an informal concert.

9. The last campaign

4 The newly arrived carrier *Bon Homme Richard* (CV-31) pulls into formation behind the veteran *Hornet*. Two *Independence* class light carriers are in the background. The picture was taken onboard the *Hornet* on 12 June 1945, which means that she is steaming with her forward flight deck bent over her bow.

5 US battleships, cruisers, and destroyers bombard the landing beaches at Okinawa. A *New Mexico* class battleship is in the foreground, with the heavy cruiser *Salt Lake City* in the background on the left.

1 On the carrier *Shangri-La*'s flight deck while at sea in the Pacific. Assistant Secretary of the Navy John L Sullivan is shown being sworn in by VADM A W Fitch, USN. The aircraft in the background are Vought F4U Corsairs.

2 Three views of refueling at sea. Although the *Iowa* class battleship is not identified, it is obviously the *Iowa* herself, after her San Francisco refit. She was the only ship of her class to carry a row of single 20mm guns on the roof of her No 2 turret. Her 3 sister-ships all carried a quad 40mm mount in this position. The oiler is the *Cahaba* (AO-82). Unfortunately the carrier is unidentified, but it is either the *Ticonderoga*, *Randolph* or *Shangri-La*.

10. Victory in the Pacific

3 The battle-scarred carrier *Franklin* (CV-13) drops anchor in New York harbor after a trip half way around the world, following the terrible damage inflicted by Japanese air attack.

3

1 The *Franklin* enters the Brooklyn Navy Yard with the help of tugs. In her wake is lower Manhattan and the Manhattan and Brooklyn Bridges. Her ensign is covering most of the damaged flight deck.

2 Starboard view of the *Franklin* at anchor in New York's lower harbour. Despite a lot of rust and damage, her overall paint scheme of Navy Blue is still evident. The three odd-colored blanks under her island mark the positions where out-board 40mm quad mounts had been mounted. They had to be removed to enable the carrier to fit through the Panama Canal.

3 Two views of the famous *Enterprise* as she heads for the Panama Canal, en route to the Navy Day celebrations in New York Harbor (25 October 1945).

4 Personnel inspection onboard the battleship *Missouri* as she heads for the Canal from Pearl Harbor. Like the *Enterprise*, she is en route to New York for Navy Day. Camouflage paint has already been removed from the battleship's wooden decks.

4

1

2

1 The battleship *Washington* and carrier *Enterprise* at the Panama Canal en route to east coast of the United States. Unfortunately the photograph's overall color is too blue.

2 Two views of the battleship *New York* as she enters New York harbor to celebrate Navy Day. The old veteran was built in New York, served with the British Grand Fleet in World War 1, and fought in both the Atlantic and the Pacific during World War 2. After the war, the tough *New York* survived both atom bomb test explosions at Bikini, but finally succumbed to numerous bombs, torpedoes and shell hits from US warships and aircraft. Thus, *New York*'s participation in the Navy Day celebration was her 'last day in the sun'.

7. Leyte The US Return to the Philippines, September 1944–January 1945

The *South Dakota* took this picture of the burning *Essex*, hit during the massive kamikaze attack on TF-38 on 25 November 1944. *Essex* was repaired at Ulithi. This was the only time that this pioneer carrier was damaged by enemy action. This picture was just one of an entire series which showed the kamikaze dive and subsequent explosion.

On 26 August 1944, Admiral 'Bull' Halsey took over command of the Fifth Fleet from Admiral Spruance, the naval forces being redesignated Third Fleet in accordance with the rotation of command. Admiral Mitscher retained direct command of the fast carriers.

Meanwhile, details were being worked out for the liberation of the Philippines. Japan was well aware that an American seizure of the Philippines would effectively end the flow of precious oil from the southern empire. The Philippines were a key link in the island chain which provided a natural security perimeter behind which merchant ships passed to and from the homeland. US submarines were constantly disrupting the movement of supplies along the chain, but the close proximity of each link's naval and air bases made these attacks risky and costly.

The major links to the north of the Philippines were Formosa and the Ryukus (Okinawa). *By-passing* and isolating Japanese strong-points had proved to be a highly successful tactic and this policy dictated that the Philippines also should be by-passed. However, the decision to liberate this large group of heavily fortified islands was largely political. It was deemed essential to American prestige not to by-pass the Philippine people. The combined strength of the United States Army and Navy was therefore committed to a single course of action.

But Japan was unaware of her enemy's intentions. As such, a number of 'Sho' plans were prepared which provided for the defense of each link in the chain. The Japanese leaders believed that they would be able to correctly anticipate America's next invasion sufficiently far in advance. However, Admiral Halsey played havoc with the Japanese plans as TF-38 ran up and down the entire chain, destroying each link's aircraft defenses piecemeal. This put all of the 'Sho' plans in trouble from the very beginning. Firstly, the majority of Japanese air power throughout the chain was knocked out before the battle even began. Secondly, they were not able to forecast the invasion location until after it was too late. Thirdly, the 'Sho' plans dictate to respond quickly was delayed until additional aircraft could be flown down from Japan.

Once the Japanese were convinced that the invasion of Leyte Gulf was for real, they set an elaborate plan in motion which would involve all of their available combat ships. The stage was now set for the world's largest naval engagement—the Battle for Leyte Gulf.

Despite exhausting and continuous operations for the

weeks preceding the battle, the US Navy had the power and balanced team needed to win. While the Japanese had the power, they did not have the teamwork. The lack of coordination between their air forces and ships would result in the useless sacrificing of hundreds of valuable planes and their aircrews. When the Japanese Navy came in for the kill, their warships were without air cover and exposed to continuous air attacks. Even when the Japanese were given a once-in-a-lifetime opportunity to break through the weak US defenses off Samar, their powerful Center Force withdrew instead. They were without air reconnaissance and as such were totally unaware of their advantageous position.

The Battle for Leyte Gulf was fought with nearly every type of ship, boat, aircraft, tactic, and operation imaginable. For example: the last battleship-versus-battleship engagement, the last carrier-versus-carrier battle, submarines against surface ships, destroyer and PT boat attacks (both day and night), battleships against escort carriers, and the introduction of suicide planes (kamikazes). In addition, the battle covered thousands of square miles of ocean. Japan believed that the fate of the nation rested on the outcome of this giant battle. When it was over, the Imperial Japanese Navy ceased to exist as an effective fighting force. *And the chain was broken.*

Although the Japanese were convincingly defeated, they fought on fanatically. They had only one weapon left—their desire to die for the emperor. This translated into the kamikaze. Convinced that Americans were too soft to go 'all the way', some Japanese felt that they could still overcome an enemy who wanted desperately to live, by proving to him that they would kill themselves in the act of killing him. Some of the pictures in this chapter, especially of the *Intrepid*, reflect this new concept of warfare. It is only the beginning, for the tempo of kamikaze attacks will increase in the operations covered in the next 2 chapters.

Navy Combat Photographers took a tremendous number of pictures during the operations which led up to, and included, the liberation of the Philippines. This is the largest single chapter in this book, but even then, just a small number of the available pictures have been included. It was difficult to make the final selection and for this reason only a handful of ships were chosen to be featured, some in moments of glory, others in times of extreme peril. The *Intrepid* filled both of these catagories. While many pictures were taken by her, numerous other pictures were also taken of her, by other ships.

Securing island bases

15 September 1944
Leyte Gulf was chosen for the landings in the Philippines, but before the major invasion took place a number of island bases were thought necessary. Assaults on Morotai and Peleliu were launched on 15 September, followed on the 23rd by the occupation of Ulithi, which became a major fleet anchorage.

Deck crashes
One of the *Enterprise*'s Helldivers crashed into the carrier's island on 2 September. While the plane was a total loss, the crew got out unharmed. The *Enterprise* was a unit of TG-38.4 with the *Franklin*, *Belleau Wood* and *San Jacinto*.

The carrier *Intrepid* back with TF-38 off the Philippines with the battleship *Iowa* in the background. On the 12 and 13 September TF-38 struck the Central Philippines with devastating results. A total of 478 Japanese aircraft were destroyed and 59 ships were sunk, with minimal Third Fleet losses. As a unit of TG-38.2, *Intrepid* operated with the *Bunker Hill*, *Cabot* and *Independence*.

This photograph had no ship identification, but it was easy to identify both ships by the camouflage patterns and their appearance details.

Peleliu assault

Guns aboard the light cruiser *Miami* in the process of getting washed down after bombarding Peleliu Island on 7 September 1944.

The Palaus were invaded on 15 September 1944, as LSM(R)s fire rockets at the beach. The First Marine Division fought a ferocious battle for the Palaus, especially on Peleliu.

Hellcats in collision

100

1 First of a 3-picture series of the barrier crash of a Hellcat on the light carrier *Cowpens* on 21 September 1944. The Hellcat's prop caught in the barrier wire, causing the fighter to flip over. While it is difficult to see in the shadows under the wing, crewmen are working to free the pilot, then clear the flight deck of the wreckage.

2 Suddenly another Hellcat comes in before the first Hellcat is cleared. Its wing will hit the crane at the left. Note that the upside-down Hellcat's wings have been folded.

3 The second Hellcat, after hitting *Cowpen's* island, comes to a stop. A crewman is tumbling away from the plane which just missed killing him. Both planes bounced on landing—thereby missing the arrestor wires.

On this day TF-38 struck at Luzon in the Philippines, destroying 300 Japanese planes and 35 merchantmen. The entire sweep through the Philippines cost the enemy 1,000 planes and 150 ships while TF-38 lost only 54 aircraft, including 18 operationally as noted in these 3 pictures.

A Hellcat taxis up *Ticonderoga*'s flight deck after having its tailhook released from the wire. The Hellcat overhead was 'waved off' because of number 53's position on the deck. Note number 56's lowered tailhook.

Ticonderoga

On 8 October, TF-38 moved into the Philippine Sea to refuel. Meanwhile, the brand new *Essex* class carrier *Ticonderoga* was working up out of Pearl Harbor. This picture has been reproduced before, but never included all of the carrier's topside radars. The fighter is a Grumman Hellcat.

Formosan air offensive

12-14 October 1944.
A massive 3-day series of air strikes was launched against Japanese airpower on Formosa. Some 600 Japanese aircraft were destroyed, and the counter-attack could only damage the carrier *Franklin* and the cruisers *Canberra* and *Houston*.

Hornet aircraft preparing to launch the first strike against Nansei Soto on 10 October. TF-38 had hit Okinawa the day before and destroyed 100 planes and 10 ships against the loss of 21 aircraft.

The big strike

Helldivers aboard the *Lexington* on 12 October 1944. TF-38 had now moved off Formosa and proceeded to sweep that large island and decimate its land-based air fleet. Admiral Halsey's intention was to destroy any potential air opposition prior to the invasion of the Philippines.

TBF Avengers returning to the *Lexington* after striking Formosa on 12 October. Each plane is rushed forward to be sent below on the forward elevator. 1,378 sorties were flown from the US carriers on the 12th.

1

2

Houston and *Canberra* torpedoed

1 Onboard the light cruiser *Houston* on 14 October 1944, after a Japanese aerial torpedo struck her engineering spaces. The starboard catapult is about to slip over the side. One day earlier, the heavy cruiser *Canberra* had also been torpedoed. Both cruisers were dead in the water and only 80 miles from Formosa. It was decided to take both ships under tow and bring them to Ulithi.

2 *Houston*'s fantail on the 16th, after a second torpedo hit the stern of the towed cruiser. The Kingfisher, crane and hatch were blown away.

Bait for Japanese surface ships

The 'bait' division under tow. The *Houston* is in the foreground with the *Canberra* in the background. The concussion caused the SK radar antenna atop the foremast to snap back.

Admiral Halsey stationed 2 carrier groups over the horizon in hope of catching a Japanese cruiser/destroyer force attempting to 'mop up' the cripples. A reconnaissance plane spotted the carriers, causing the Japanese to beat a hasty retreat.

Franklin damaged

Looking down at *Houston*'s damaged stern, with its flooded hangar.

The USS *Franklin* launching aircraft against Formosa as seen from the light carrier *San Jacinto*. On 13 October a Japanese bomber slipped across the *Franklin*'s flight deck and crashed into the sea. The same day this picture was taken (the 12th) the carrier was slightly damaged by a bomb hit.

Leyte—the first phase

20 October 1944.
The landings in Leyte Gulf were lightly opposed, but a massive naval counter-attack was prepared by the Japanese. The first stage of the resulting engagement comprised a large, land-based air attack on TF-38, sinking the carrier *Princeton*, and a counter-strike against the Japanese Center Force sinking the battleship *Musashi*. Known as the battle of the Sibuyan Sea, it took place on 24 October.

A vital key to the Fast Carrier Task Force's success was its ability to remain at sea for prolonged periods. Shown is Service Squadron 6 heading to a rendezvous point to refuel and reprovision TF-38.

The 6-day battle off Formosa was the largest air battle yet fought between carrier planes and land-based aircraft. Japan lost 600 planes and 40 ships: 154 of those lost were carrier planes from Japan's Third and Fourth Carrier Division. The US lost a total of 80 aircraft. The stage was now set for the invasion of the Philippines.

The Leyte landings

Americans back in the Philippines during the landings on Leyte Island on 20 October 1944. Coast Guardsmen and soldiers are shown filling sand bags for gun emplacements. The landings in Leyte Gulf were lightly opposed. Once the intent was clear, Japan set in motion a gigantic operation which was designed to destroy the landing ships in this picture.

The *Intrepid* off San Bernardino Strait, the Philippines, on 23 October 1944. She is in the process of receiving replacement aircraft from the escort carrier *Sargent Bay*. The opening stages of the massive Battle for Leyte Gulf were already underway as this peaceful picture was being taken. The Japanese were ferrying 450 naval aircraft from the north to the Philippines via Formosa while 2 US submarines were sinking the Japanese heavy cruisers *Atago* and *Maya* to the south (part of the Center Force).

Japanese attack on TF-38

1 *Intrepid* opened the aerial segment of the battle just after 8am on 24 October 1944, when one of her Helldivers spotted the Japanese Center Force in the Sibuyan Sea. This Helldiver just made it back to the *Intrepid* as she ran out of gas. The dive-bomber had to be pushed forward to clear the landing area.

2 Japan struck TG-38.3 on the morning of 24 October, with 3 waves of approximately 50 planes each. Only one bomber did any damage. Its bomb set off a chain reaction which led to the loss of the light carrier *Princeton* (shown with smoke pouring out of her hangar deck). The picture was taken by the *South Dakota*.

During the air battle, the US Navy's leading ace shot down 9 Japanese fighters: Commander McCampbell finished the war with a total of 34 kills.

The stricken *Princeton*

3 This unbelievable picture was taken by the light cruiser *Birmingham* as she moved alongside the dying *Princeton*. Except for 40 or 50 men, the ship had been abandoned—note the lone figure sitting atop the bridge. The devastation was caused by exploding torpedoes and bombs mounted on aircraft in the hangar. All the fires were under control except for the one near the after magazine.

4 *Birmingham*'s cameraman took this view looking at men standing on the buckled flight deck with the wrecked forward elevator behind them. Just when everything seemed to be under control, the entire after portion of the carrier blew up—everyone out in the open on either the *Princeton* or *Birmingham* was killed or wounded.

Damage to *Birmingham*

This close-up graphically illustrates the topside damage to the *Birmingham* caused by *Princeton*'s final explosion. The ship's complement of 1,200 men suffered terribly—229 were killed instantly, 420 were wounded and 4 were missing. The *Princeton* was still afloat and in no danger of sinking, but she was also still afire with night approaching. The cruiser *Reno* sank the hulk with torpedoes. *Princeton* was the last American fast carrier to be sunk by enemy action.

TF-38 hits back

Helldivers from the *Intrepid* 'joining up' over TG-38.2 before heading for the Japanese Center Force. The first strikes were launched from the *Intrepid* and the *Cabot*. By the end of the day, 259 planes had attacked the Center Force, sinking the battleship *Musashi* and damaging 3 more battleships. The enemy force then turned around and appeared to retire.

This picture is a black and white conversion from a color transparency which had deteriorated to a monochromatic red.

Battles off Samar and Cape Engano

25 October 1944.
The Japanese Southern Force was routed during the night of the 25th in Surigao Strait, but TF-38 was decoyed to attack the Northern Force off Cape Engano. This gave the Center Force a golden opportunity to disrupt the Leyte landings, a chance they dissipated attacking escort carriers off Samar.

1

The decoy works

1 General Quarters on board the *Intrepid* as TF-38 heads north to strike the Japanese carrier force on 25 October. As TF-38 rushed north, it left San Bernardino Strait unprotected. Meanwhile, the Japanese Center Force had turned around again and passed through the strait around midnight, just before the Southern Force ran into the trap waiting for them at Suriga Strait, and destruction at the hands of the US Seventh Fleet.

2

2 Onboard the light carrier *San Jacinto*, men load a torpedo on to an Avenger. The fast carriers were getting ready to attack Japan's Northern Force which was composed of 4 carriers and 2 carrier/battleships.

Taffy 3 under attack

3 A group of escort carriers and their screen, known as 'Taffy 3', came under the guns of the Japanese Center Force at first light on the 25th. This photo shows units of Taffy 3 making smoke as Japanese shells splash amidst the group.

3

The escort carrier *Gambier Bay* making smoke and taking evasive action in an attempt to dodge shells from a Japanese cruiser (just visible on the horizon at the extreme right of this picture). The picture was taken from the *Kitkun Bay*. The *Gambier Bay* had less than half an hour left to live.

The close similarity between slow American escort carriers and fast light fleet carriers caused the Japanese to mistake this escort group for TF-38. Aircraft from the 6 'jeep' carriers kept the enemy under constant attack, reinforcing the belief. Two destroyers and an escort destroyer were also sunk charging the Japanese, in an effort to protect their carriers.

Off Cape Engano

Intrepid's aircraft warming up as they prepare to finish off the Japanese carrier force off Cape Engano. There were only 29 planes left onboard the enemy carriers. TF-38 launched 6 strikes totalling 572 aircraft against the 17 Japanese ships. Urgent appeals from Taffy 3 forced Admiral Halsey to rush back to San Bernardino Strait with his battleships and *Intrepid*'s carrier group before all the enemy ships could be finished off.

A damaged Avenger (note the wing) from the *San Jacinto* took this picture of the Japanese carrier/battleship *Ise* as she turns sharply off Cape Engano. All 4 of the Northern Force's carriers, and 1 destroyer, were sunk. Both carrier/battleships, a light cruiser and several destroyers were also damaged. The Japanese Center Force withdrew before a very frustrated Halsey arrived off San Bernardino Strait, but his ships did manage to sink a retreating destroyer.

1 Onboard the light carrier *Cabot* on 26 October 1944. Both TG-38.1 and 38.2 launched a number of strikes against the retreating Japanese, sinking 1 light cruiser, 2 destroyers and damaging a heavy cruiser.

Stragglers continued to be chased down and sunk. The Battle for Leyte Gulf finished the Japanese Navy as a force to be reckoned with. Sunk during 4 days of fighting were: 4 aircraft carriers, 3 battleships, 6 heavy cruisers, 3 light cruisers and 9 destroyers. Several of the survivors would not make it out of the Philippines during the following weeks.

Casualties of the Leyte campaign

The light cruiser *Honolulu* in floating drydock ABSD-2, Manus Island on 2 November 1944. The hole in her portside bottom (just below the bridge) was caused by a Japanese aerial torpedo on 20 October 1944, while the *Honolulu* was bombarding Leyte Island during the invasion.

The anti-aircraft cruiser *Reno* dead in the water off San Bernardino Strait after being torpedoed by the Japanese submarine *I-41* on 3 November 1944. The *Reno* was towed 1,500 miles to Ulithi for temporary repairs.

Also on 3 November, TF-38 pounded Luzon and destroyed 439 Japanese planes.

The first Kamikaze attacks

The *Intrepid* buries her dead off Luzon on 29 October. She was the first *Essex* class carrier to be hit by a kamikaze. The damage did not affect her operationally. Strikes against Luzon on this day cost the Japanese 84 aircraft, against 11 US losses.

The Leyte campaign saw the first concerted use of a new Japanese terror weapon—the suicide attack or *kamikaze*. Short of trained personnel and first rate aircraft, to the Japanese it seemed a highly cost-effective method of warfare in the circumstances.

1 Units of TG-38.4 off Leyte in close support on 30 October. It was soon to be a dreadful day for 2 US carriers and a victory for 7 Japanese suicide pilots. This picture was taken from the light carrier *Belleau Wood* over an oiler and the destroyer *Mugford*, at the *Enterprise* as she came alongside an oiler.

TG-38.4 under kamikaze attack

2 As seen from the *Belleau Wood*, the *Franklin* burns after taking a kamikaze hit. A second kamikaze is directly over the *Franklin*'s island. She has just dropped a bomb which missed the burning carrier.

Imagine the horror in the minds of the men on *Belleau Wood*'s flight deck as they watched that speck above the *Franklin* get bigger and bigger as it approached their twisting ship and took aim at the 11 Hellcats parked on the carrier's fantail.

3 Both carriers now burn as crewmen work to bring the flames under control. The *Franklin* lost 56 men killed, 60 injured, and 33 aircraft destroyed. The *Belleau Wood* lost 92 killed, 54 seriously injured and 12 planes destroyed. The *Enterprise* was just missed by the last kamikaze which passed within 15 feet of the carrier's packed flight deck.

113

Lexington is hit

This 3-picture sequence shows the *Lexington* as a kamikaze slams into her island superstructure on 5 November. The resulting explosion and fires killed 50 and injured 132. The 'Lex' was repaired at Ulithi. The day before she was hit, her planes sank the heavy cruiser *Nachi* (one of the survivors from the Battle for Leyte Gulf).

Essex and *Ticonderoga*

A flak-damaged Avenger folds its wings as it taxis forward on *Essex*'s flight deck on 5 November. The plane appears to be in pretty good shape, but take a good look at the rear gunner's position. The ball turret has been smashed and there is a large jagged hole aft of the turret. The gunner had been killed instantly, but the rest of the crew got out of the plane. Funeral services were performed immediately and the entire plane was 'buried at sea'.

The *Essex* took this picture on 5 November, as a kamikaze crashes alongside the newly arrived *Ticonderoga*.

Luzon strikes resumed

At MacArthur's request, carrier air strikes against Luzon were resumed on 13 November 1944. Concentrating on Japanese planes and seaborne reinforcements, the raids were highly successful.

The *Essex* refuels from the oiler *Tallulah* off Luzon on 13 November 1944. Manila Bay was hit on this day and 1 light cruiser, 4 destroyers, and 7 merchantmen were sunk.

The *Intrepid* on her way back to the Philippines after a brief rest at Ulithi.

Units of the Japanese Center Force were retreating north of Formosa on 21 November when they ran into the sub *Sealion*. She sank both the battleship *Kongo* and the destroyer *Urakaze*.

1

2

1 One of *Intrepid*'s escorts alongside the carrier. The distinctive camouflage pattern of the battleship *Iowa*, with a destroyer alongside, can be seen in the background.

2 *Intrepid* aircraft get ready to launch strikes against the Philippines after spending a quiet Thanksgiving Day at sea.

The planes closest to the camera are Hellcats with Helldivers behind them

TF-38 hit Luzon and sank another heavy cruiser (a straggler from the Battle for Leyte Gulf), plus 7 other ships, and destroyed 55 planes. However, a large number of kamikazes were on their way to hit the Fast Carrier Force.

Kamikaze victory

25 November 1944.
The Japanese counter to the Luzon strikes was the largest and most determined kamikaze attack to date. The carriers were the main target, and 3 were hit—*Intrepid* (twice), *Hancock* and *Cabot*. Only *Intrepid* was badly damaged but TF-38 withdrew to Ulithi.

The ordeal of the *Intrepid*

1 The *Intrepid* turns sharply as her gunners shoot down a Betty heavy bomber on 25 November. While this was happening another kamikaze exploded directly over the *Hancock*, showering her with burning debris and starting several fires.

2 *Intrepid*'s turn came just minutes after the *Hancock* caught it. Seen from the *Cabot*, a burning kamikaze aims for *Intrepid*'s flight deck. The wake between the 2 carriers is from the *New Jersey*.

First hit

These 3 pictures were taken from the *New Jersey* as her men watch the *Intrepid* take her first kamikaze hit. Note that the men in the lower portion of the picture are totally unaware of *Intrepid*'s plight because their view is blocked by the 40mm mount in front of them.

Second hit

1 The *Intrepid* burns from her first kamikaze hit as crewmen watch another Japanese plane heading toward their damaged ship.

2 The second kamikaze slams into the *Intrepid* about 75 feet aft of where the first one had hit only minutes before. Note the wood flight deck planking in mid-air. This kamikaze's bomb penetrated the flight deck and exploded in the hangar.

3 *Intrepid*'s flight deck and hangar blazed for 2 hours while her crew fought to contain the fire and save their ship. (This negative has a number of scratches and marks on it.)

Cabot and *Essex* hit

While both the *Hancock* and *Intrepid* burned, the kamikazes continued to come in. The *Cabot* was hit next, by a direct hit and a near miss. A lone Avenger sits defiantly on *Cabot's* flight deck, surrounded by smoke, debris and worried men.

Last to be hit was the *Essex*. While the picture is blurred, it clearly shows the kamikaze diving on the carrier.

The hit on the *Essex* looked worse than it actually was, especially when viewed from her port side, as *Ticonderoga*'s photographer took this picture. The kamikaze hit the port side overhang. No damage was received internally.

Aftermath

Four Hellcats fly over the smoldering *Intrepid* as her men inspect the damage. The *New Jersey* is barely visible in the distance, just to the right of the lone Hellcat parked forward. During the attack on 25 November 32 kamikazes were destroyed, but the damage to TF-38 forced Halsey to break off and retire.

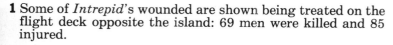

1

1 Some of *Intrepid*'s wounded are shown being treated on the flight deck opposite the island: 69 men were killed and 85 injured.

2 The hole caused by the first kamikaze (and its bomb) to hit the *Intrepid*. The wounded men being treated in the previous photo are visible in the background.

3 The cameraman moved further aft to snap the holes made by the second kamikaze, its outline clearly visible in the deck. The round hole closest to the camera was where the bomb penetrated *Intrepid*'s flight deck. A view of the first hole is blocked by the men surrounding this hole.

4 Her crew begins to clean up the debris in *Intrepid*'s hangar as some of their dead shipmates are removed for burial. Because of her substantial damage, the *Intrepid* would have to be repaired on the West Coast. The *Intrepid* and her sister carriers of TF-38 amassed a formidable battle record during the month of November—against 97 planes lost and 5 carriers damaged, Japan suffered 675 aircraft destroyed, 40 ships sunk and the total failure of numerous attempts to reinforce the Philippines.

3

4

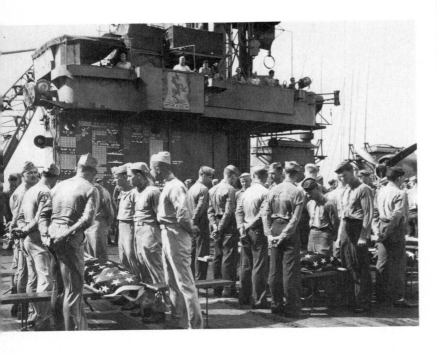

The *Cabot* buries her dead as she returns to Ulithi with TF-38 on 26 November. Three days later, while the US Fast Carrier Force rested and licked its wounds, the submarine *Archerfish* sank Japan's newest and largest carrier, the not-yet-completed *Shinano*, off Tokyo Bay.

Leyte is secured

The Islands of Leyte and Samar were considered 'secured' by Christmas Day, but the decision to invade Luzon via Mindoro had already been taken. TF-38 was again called upon to support the landings.

A short rest

TF-38 at rest in Ulithi lagoon on 8 December 1944. This carrier line-up was nicknamed 'murderer's row'. From front to back: *Ticonderoga, Hancock, Hornet, Yorktown* and *Wasp*.

Further Luzon strikes

Admiral McCain's flagship, the *Hancock*, off Luzon on 16 December. TG-38.2 had been reorganized to include the *Hancock*, *Lexington* (Admiral Mitscher's former flagship), *Hornet*, *Cabot* and *Independence*.

A Hellcat warming up in front of *Hancock*'s island on 16 December. TF-38 fighter sweeps destroyed 269 Japanese aircraft, against 28 US planes lost over the target and another 38 lost operationally, during the period 14-16 December.

The *New Jersey* leads TF-38 out of Ulithi on 11 December and heads for Luzon to support the coming invasion of Mindoro.

5

3

6

Typhoon

1 An unidentified *Sumner* class destroyer alongside the *Hancock* in deteriorating weather. After 3 days of high-speed carrier operations, many of TF-38's ships were low on fuel. Halsey intended to refuel them on 17 December and then resume strikes on the 19th. (The light scratches across this picture are in the original negative.)

2 A *Fletcher* class destroyer plows past the carrier *Wasp* as the storm worsens on 17 December. The weather got so bad that fueling had to be postponed while the task force attempted to evade the storm—but to no avail.

What the Japanese Navy had been unable to do, the weather did for them, A fully-fledged typhoon hit TF-38 on 18 December. Three destroyers rolled over and sank, 146 aircraft were destroyed, 20 ships were damaged and approximately 800 men lost their lives.

3 TF-38 returned to Ulithi without hitting Luzon again because the typhoon was now over the island. This picture was taken from the *Essex* as her task group (TG-38.3) enters Ulithi. The 5 visible ships are (front to back): the light carrier *Langley*, the carrier *Ticonderoga* and the battleships *Washington*, *North Carolina* and *South Dakota*.

While the Fast Carrier Force licked its wounds on 19 December, after the typhoon, the 'silent service' continued to smite the Japanese Navy as the *Redfish* sank the new carrier *Unryu*.

The fleet anchorage

4 *New Jersey* men relax on their flagship as the holidays approach. Christmas would be spent in Ulithi but the New Year would find them back at sea.

5 Christmas Day on the *Lexington*. The ship's company is lined up to receive decorations from their commanding officer. The *Lexington* completed repairs from her kamikaze hits and was made Rear Admiral Bogan's flagship of TG-38.2 on 11 December 1944.

6 The mighty battleship *Iowa* enters floating drydock ABSD-2. She was on her way to a major overhaul on the West Coast.

Lingayen Gulf

9 January 1945.
The invasion of Luzon began with a fiercely opposed landing at Lingayen Gulf. Kamikazes were again very busy, and ship casualties were heavy. Nevertheless this was the beginning of the end for the Japanese on Luzon, although a number of subsidiary operations—like the assault on Corregidor—were still necessary.

1

Kamikazes hit the escort carriers

1 On 3 and 5 January 1945, TG-77.4 was hit by several kamikazes while on the way to Lingayen Gulf. The escort carrier *Ommaney Bay* was sunk and the *Manila Bay* (shown) was damaged. This picture was taken by the battleship *West Virginia*.

2 This picture was taken a few seconds after the kamikaze crashed into the *Manila Bay* (at the base of the island) on 5 January. (The negative is heavily scratched.)

3 A kamikaze flies past the stern of the escort carrier *Steamer Bay* on 5 January. Three days later the *Kadashan Bay* and the *Kitkun Bay* were damaged by kamikazes.

Lingayen Gulf

4 The Australian heavy cruiser *Shropshire*, in Lingayen Gulf, fires at Luzon prior to the amphibious assault.

5 *LSM-14* landing equipment during the invasion of Luzon on 9 January 1945. At the same time TF-38 hit Formosa and then moved into the South China Sea.

2

Mosquito fleet

6 A nest of US PT boats in the Philippines during February 1945. While generally unsuited for most Pacific operations, these boats were especially valuable in the Philippines and the South Pacific.

Corregidor

7 Corregidor was assaulted on 16 February. Landing craft pass the island as C-47 troop transports drop paratroopers on 'The Rock' and its 5,000 defenders.

8 *PT-375* glides past Corregidor on 16 February with a number of paratroopers who had become isolated and trapped by the Japanese. It took 10 days to clear the maze of tunnels and caves. On 2 March, General MacArthur raised the American flag over the island.

3

4

5

6

7

8

8. The Winter Campaigns

From the South China Sea to Iwo Jima, January-March 1945

After spending Christmas at Ulithi, Admiral Halsey took the Third Fleet back to sea on 30 December 1944. While the Seventh Fleet continued operations to secure the remainder of the Philippines, TF-38 struck north at Formosa and Okinawa. The purpose of these repeat raids was to knock out the new planes which were in the process of being ferried down from Japan to reinforce the Philippines. For example, the carrier strikes of 3 and 4 January destroyed 111 planes parked in staging areas. They would never reach Luzon (northern Philippines).

On 9 January, the day the Seventh Fleet invaded Luzon, TF-38 steamed into the South China Sea to hunt for Japanese ships and planes. Against virtually no opposition, the fast carriers swept the harbors and waters off Indo-China. After leaving what had once been considered a Japanese lake (South China Sea), TF-38 again hit the air-craft staging areas on Formosa. America's fast carriers were now roaming Japan's inner security perimeter at will.

Back at Ulithi, rotation of command ceremonies reinsti-tuted Admiral Spruance as fleet commander and Admiral Mitscher as Task Force commander. TF-58 then put to sea and headed for Tokyo. This was the first carrier strike to hit the enemy mainland since Doolittle's raid, almost 3 years earlier. The remnants of the Japanese Navy made no attempt to intervene. American Hellcats and Corsairs cleared the skies of all fighter opposition. While Japan itself was under attack, the assault against Iwo Jima began. The fast carriers then positioned themselves between Japan and Iwo, supporting the invasion to the southeast, blocking reinforcements from the west and then hitting Japan with a second series of air raids. This time, the strikes were actually the opening stages of the invasion of Okinawa. It was during this operation off the enemy's coast that the saga of the *Franklin* was written. Even though the story has been told many times we felt that the viewer would want to see some of the *Franklin* pictures which have not been seen before, plus one or two 'printed earlier' exceptions to round out the story.

As with previous chapters, we have reproduced a number of aircraft crashes. They only serve to highlight the hazards of landing an airplane, especially a battle-damaged one, on the moving deck of a ship. Known as operational casualties, the frequency of these crashes was minimal, especially when compared to the number of combat sorties.

Most of the photography taken during this period was strikingly beautiful, especially the underway views of ships either plowing through choppy waters or gliding over silvery smooth seas. The peaceful scenes are sharply contrasted with action pictures which graphically illustrate planes crashing, ships burning, and men dying. Again, the camera has allowed us to look back in time and put our-selves into the middle of the contradiction of war, as experi-enced by American sailors in the Pacific. A few of the action pictures are out of focus. This only emphasizes the violence of battle, as captured by the combat camera.

Amphibious tanks, holding some of the 40,000 Marines destined to be ashore by nightfall, head for their assigned beaches on Iwo Jima. The battleships *Tennessee* and *Nevada* are providing fire support with several destroyers firing point blank into the island. The soon-to-be dreaded Mount Suribachi is the large mound to the right of center. Four days after this picture was taken the US Marines placed the American flag on top of the mount. The picture was taken from the battleship *West Virginia*.

South China Sea

January 1945.
In support of the Luzon campaign, Halsey took the Third Fleet into the South China Sea, and in a series of attacks on targets from Formosa to Camranh Bay, sank over 130,000 tons of shipping and destroyed several hundred airplanes.

This picture was taken from the *New Jersey* as the destroyer *English* moves through a choppy sea. The *Hancock* is the carrier in the background. TF-38 had just completed 2 days of strikes on Formosa, destroying 111 planes and 16 ships while losing 22 aircraft.

The *English* about to cross just behind *New Jersey*'s fantail. *Hancock* and the newly returned *Enterprise* are following. The *Enterprise* joined TF-38 on 5 January 1945 as night carrier with 45 radar-equipped Hellcats and Avengers.

1 The *Lexington* refueling in the South China Sea. TF-38 was looking for stragglers from the Battle of Leyte Gulf, particularly the carrier/battleships *Ise* and *Hyuga*.

2 Some of the 101 ships of TF-38 in the South China Sea, as seen from the *Hornet*. The *Stephen Potter* is refueling alongside an unidentified oiler. The familiar silhouette on the horizon is the *Hancock*.

3 Onboard the *Hancock*: this Hellcat was damaged over Indochina by anti-aircraft fire and burst into flame when it landed. The pilot died the next day.

While in the South China Sea, TF-38 sank 56 ships and destroyed 181 aircraft against a loss of 62 planes.

Contrasting weather conditions

TF-38 pushes through some nasty weather off the Coast of China. Despite this, several aircraft are in the air. It is easy to understand why photographers rarely bothered to take any pictures when the weather was poor.

Hancock's photographer captured the early morning activity on the flagship's flight deck at the beginning of another day of operations. Meanwhile, operations have just ended on the night carrier *Enterprise* (almost invisible in the background).

A Hellcat passes over the *Hancock* as a Helldiver warms up on the flight deck. Units of *Hancock's* Task Group (TG-38.2) also included the carriers *Hornet* (shown) and *Lexington*.

Deck accidents

A damaged Hellcat which came in too high, missed the barrier and slammed down on the flight deck, breaking a wheel as the prop tore up the flight deck's wood planking. The fighter came to a stop against *Bataan*'s island. Taken in the South China Sea on 18 January.

This Hellcat pilot has reason to smile. His plane is a total wreck—he almost went over the side into the sea—but he is unharmed. Taken onboard the light carrier *Bataan* in the South China Sea.

21 January 1945

The Japanese reply to TF-38's strikes was the usual kamikaze air attacks, the carriers *Ticonderoga* and *Langley* being hit. *Hancock* was also damaged, but from a flight deck accident.

Ticonderoga is hit twice

The *Ticonderoga* takes a kamikaze on her flight deck the day after TF-38 left the South China Sea (21 January 1945). Fortunately, the plane crashed on the empty deck forward instead of the packed deck aft.

Forty minutes after the first kamikaze hit the *Ticonderoga*, another one crashed into the island's forward director. This picture was taken seconds after the plane hit and exploded.

Down, but not out

1 *Essex* men watch the bleeding *Ticonderoga* as smoke pours out of her port side hangar. Most of the fires are now under control. Her personnel losses were the heaviest to date: 143 killed and 202 injured.

2 *Ticonderoga*'s wrecked director. Note the splinter screen peeled back against the tripod and smoke stack and the splinter damage to the stack. The carrier's damage was more than compensated for by the destruction of 106 enemy planes and 10 ships off Formosa during strikes on 21 January 1945.

Hancock disaster

The *Hancock* also suffered on the 21st, but not from the Japanese. An Avenger made a normal landing and was taxiing past the island when it blew up, spraying the surrounding flight deck with debris. Evidently, a 500lb bomb carried by the plane exploded killing the plane's crew instantly.

This picture is indicative of the carnage on *Hancock*'s flight deck after the Avenger exploded. The wounded have been moved to sick bay but the bodies of 5 dead still remain. The Avenger's engine came to a stop just forward of the 5in mounts, next to the covered remains of one of *Hancock*'s men.

Heading back to Ulithi

Essex aircraft warm up on the flight deck. The planes are Corsairs, Hellcats and Avengers. All of the *Essex*'s Hell-diver dive-bombers were put ashore before the carrier left Ulithi on 30 December 1944. She now carried 90 fighters, 36 of them were the latest Corsairs—piloted by US Marine pilots.

TF-38 becomes TF-58

27 January 1945.
Admiral Spruance took over from Halsey and TF-38 became TF-58. The Fifth Fleet's task was ultimately to support the Iwo Jima landing (19 February), but on 16-17 February the Fleet carried out the first carrier raid on the mainland of Japan since Doolittle's in 1942.

Resting at Ulithi

Two of *Hornet*'s men look over some of the units of the powerful US Navy at Ulithi. The carriers in this picture are (front to back): *Wasp*, *Hancock*, and *Essex*.

The battleship *New Jersey* shows the strain of long operations as she lies at anchor in Ulithi Atoll on 8 February 1945. Taken from the seaplane tender *Chandeleur*.

Also taken by the *Chandeleur* on the same day, this view shows the newly arrived fleet carriers *Randolph* (foreground) and *Bennington*.

TF-58 sails

Units of TF-58 depart Ulithi on 12 February, en route to strike Japan. As seen from the *Wasp*, the ships are the destroyer *De Haven*, light cruiser *Vicksburg* and the newly returned *Belleau Wood*. They were part of a task force which now included 166 ships.

Preparing for the Tokyo strike

Aboard the *Essex* at the end of the day. Hellcats and Corsairs stand ready to make the first strike against Japan since Doolittle's raid on Tokyo. The profile in the distance belongs to the light cruiser *Wilkes-Barre*.

Taken from the *Hancock*, over an oiler and destroyer, at the light cruiser *Pasadena* and the battleship *New Jersey*. The sea is mirror-smooth.

Missing the wire

1 This Helldiver bounced upon landing and missed 'the wire'. The camera caught the plane just as its landing gear snared the crash barrier. Those reproduced have been selected from a sequence of over 20 taken aboard the *Randolph*. The plane was returning after striking Japan on 17 February 1945.

2 Stopped by the crash barrier, the Helldiver's nose digs into the deck as the fuselage caves in behind the engine.

3 The Helldiver falls back on its tailwheel as the ruptured gas lines explode and cover the plane's crew with flames. *Randolph*'s firefighters rush to aid the 2 men trapped in the plane. Note the man with hose coming from the lower left.

4 As other firefighters spray the burning plane, the man in the previous shot still waits for his hose to be turned on. Two men in asbestos suits are helping the rear gunner to get out of the plane.

5 The pilot walks away from his burning plane, apparently unhurt. The man with the hose has moved away from the wheel and continues to wait.

6 As additional firefighters arrive, the man finally gets his hose going. Note the specially designed spray and fog nozzles used to reach aircraft fires.

The strikes go on

Hornet crewmen enjoy a cigarette and coffee break in a 40mm gun tub between strikes against Japan on 16 and 17 February. It was a drastic change from warm Ulithi to the cold Northern Pacific.

Hellcat fighters ready to launch off the *Yorktown* on 17 February. They are armed with 5in rockets carried under their wings.

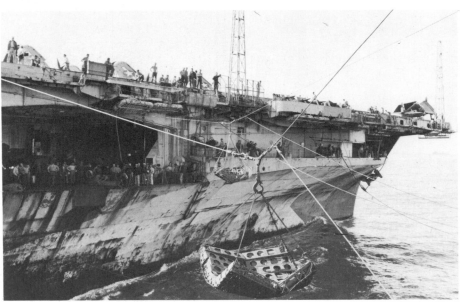

The *Hornet* receives a load of 100lb bombs from the ammunition ship *Shasta* after the strikes against Japan. TF-58 was now on its way to hit Iwo Jima and cover the invasion of that island. The strikes against Japan were designed to reduce the enemy's ability to respond instantly to the assault on Iwo Jima.

Iwo Jima

19 February 1945.
Iwo Jima was invaded after the heaviest ever
bombardment by ships and planes—but to no avail.
The island took over a month to secure, and the epic
battle has rightly become part of Marine Corps
legend.

Pre-assault bombardment

1 The newly arrived battleship *New York* fires at Iwo Jima as
the assault begins on 19 February 1945.

2 Men aboard the battleship *Nevada* watch the action on Iwo
Jima as the landing craft head for the beach. The *Nevada*
had been one of those ships which was sunk at Pearl Harbor
over 3 years earlier.

Beachhead carnage

A section of the beach where the Marines stormed ashore on Iwo Jima as it appeared 2 days after the landings. The dead have been removed but the wreckage of the battle remains.

Saratoga

The night carrier *Saratoga* on the way to take up station off Iwo Jima and provide night air cover. Escort carriers would provide the day air support.

Rows of dead (in white canvas bags) on the deck of an LST which was quickly converted into a hospital ship off Iwo Jima.

1 'Sara' crewmen relax against the carrier's large smoke stack. On 21 February these same men would be manning the guns they are now playing checkers on—and fighting for their lives. In a space of 3 minutes, the *Saratoga* would be hit by 5 kamikazes and bombs. A second attack would hit her with another kamikaze and bomb.

2 *Saratoga* men look for the remains of some of their shipmates in the holes caused by the fourth kamikaze to hit the carrier. The white substance on the deck is firefighting foam. A total of 123 men were killed and 192 were injured; 42 of her planes were destroyed or ditched because they had no place to land.

3 While the rest of 'Sara's' topsides were a shambles, her island was totally intact, except for some blistered paint. America's oldest carrier would spend the next few months in a shipyard and be as good as new. This was the third and last time that she would receive damage at the hands of the Japanese.

Saratoga's replacement

Aboard the *Enterprise* off Iwo Jima on 7 March 1945. The 'Big E' remained on station as *Saratoga*'s replacement until 10 March. During this assignment, the *Enterprise* kept planes over the target for 174 continuous hours, non-stop. This Avenger's damaged landing gear collapsed as it touched down.

1 Units of TF-58 refuel on 23 February as they head back to Japan for a second series of strikes. *Lexington*'s camera looks over an oiler's stack, the heavy cruiser *Baltimore*'s fantail and the destroyer *Cushing*. The heavy cruiser *Pittsburgh* and the carrier *Hancock* are in the background.

2 Ernie Pyle being transferred from the light carrier *Cabot* by breeches-buoy to the destroyer *Moalt*. America's most famous war correspondent had only a month to live when this picture was taken. A sniper's bullet took his life during the Okinawa campaign, on the island of Le Shima.

3 Avengers and Helldivers from the *Bunker Hill* fly over Okinawa's coastline on 1 March 1945. The weather off Japan was so miserable that Admiral Mitscher was forced to move down to Okinawa as the secondary target.

4 An Avenger gets its wing chopped off by *Bunker Hill*'s after 5in gun mounts as it makes a bad landing after striking Okinawa. These were the first strikes against Nakijima Ota and Koizimi.

Okinawa strike

A further strike against the Japanese mainland by TF-58 was planned, but bad weather intervened, and Okinawa—which was to be the next invasion target—was attacked instead. This was followed by a rest period at Ulithi, during which a daring kamikaze raid was carried out on the fleet anchorage.

1

3

2

4

A spectacular accident

One of the most incredible pictures taken during World War 2 by a US Navy Combat Photographer. A Hellcat smashes into 6 other Hellcats parked forward on *Cowpen*'s flight deck as crewmen duck and run for cover (on the left). The camera captured all the debris in mid-air. Note that there are pilots in the parked Hellcats.

Seconds after the crash, men rush up to the wrecked Hellcats to help the pilots.

Ulithi

The *Enterprise* arrives back at Ulithi to join the rest of the Fast Carrier Task Force. The planes on deck are all radar-equipped Hellcats and Avengers (note wing domes). The new battlecruiser *Alaska* is following the carrier into the anchorage.

The *Enterprise* passes the *Yorktown* (center) *Hornet* (left) and *Randolph* (behind *Yorktown*'s bow) as she moves to her anchorage and a much deserved rest. A couple of hours after this picture was taken the *Randolph* was hit by a long range kamikaze.

Strike

The hole in *Randolph* as seen on the morning after (12 March) she was hit: 25 men were killed, 106 were wounded. *Randolph* was repaired at her anchorage and resumed operations by the first week of April, off Okinawa. The bomber which hit the *Randolph* was one of 24 which made up a special suicide unit for the attack on Ulithi. Only one got through to do any damage.

TF-58 at Ulithi on 13 March, the day before they sailed to resume operations against the Japanese. The ships in the nearest row are (left to right): *Intrepid*, *Enterprise*, *Yorktown*, an unidentified *Independence*, the damaged *Randolph* and the battleship *Massachusetts*. This picture's location was incorrectly given as Guam.

against Japan

The strike against the mainland that was cancelled in February was carried out in March. TF-58 came under heavy air attack—the most serious raid damaged *Wasp* and *Intrepid* and nearly sank *Franklin*.

Strike force

Units of TG-58.4 on their way to strike Japan. The group consisted of the 3 large carriers shown: the *Yorktown* in the foreground, *Enterprise* in the center, and the *Intrepid* in the background.

Intrepid prepares a strike

Corsairs and Helldivers being moved forward as *Intrepid* prepares to launch strikes against Kyushu on 18 March 1945.

1

2

154

1 *Intrepid* launches its aircraft. This picture is also a black and white conversion. Sixteen Japanese warships were damaged on 19 March.

TF-58 refuels

2 A *Bennington* crewman looks over the light cruiser *Miami* as they refuel from a fleet oiler. The carrier refueling in the background is the *Wasp*.

Lucky escape for the *Enterprise*

3 The *Enterprise* had a very close call on 18 March. A 500lb bomb hit the port side of the island and failed to explode. This picture vividly shows how the dud bounced across the flight deck, spilling explosives. The bomb casing is at the upper right corner. It was thrown overboard. Forty minutes later, the *Intrepid* was hit.

18 March

4 The light carrier *Langley* took this picture of what appears to be a Japanese plane exploding against *Intrepid*'s starboard side. Actually, the plane would have hit the carrier had a 5in shell not blown off the heavy bomber's tail and caused the plane to veer off and crash in the water.

3

4

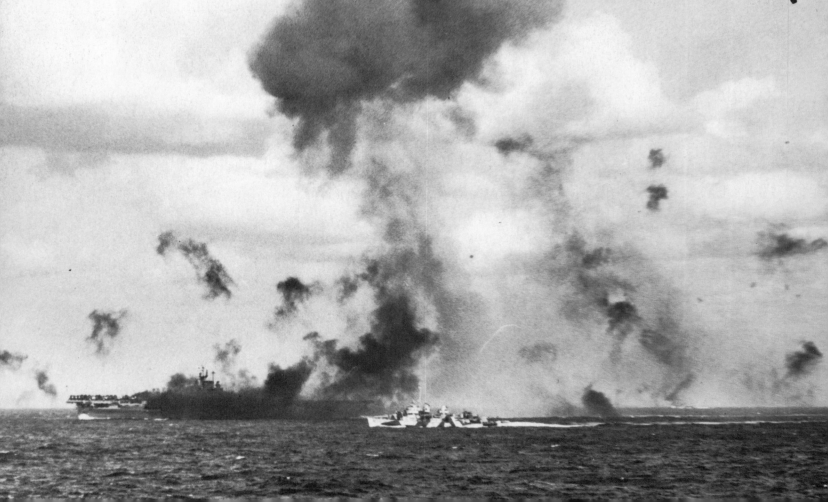

1 This photo was taken by the light cruiser *Santa Fe*, seconds after the previous shot was taken by the *Langley*. As the bomber exploded only 50 feet off the *Intrepid* it showered the carrier with flaming gas and debris. Smoke is already pouring out of the hangar deck. Ships on *Intrepid*'s starboard side were convinced that the carrier had been blown up.

2 Back on the *Langley*, smoke pours from the burning *Intrepid* raising a large cloud astern of the carrier. Damage control quickly put out the fires without affecting operations.

3 A radar-equipped Hellcat about to land on the *Enterprise* on 18 March during a Japanese air raid. This view shows the wires which had to be hooked in order to land safely aboard.

19 March—*Essex* near-missed

Off the coast of Kyushu the Fast Carrier Task Force came under repeated air attack on 19 March 1944. Men on the light carrier *Cabot* watch as a kamikaze aims for the *Essex*.

The *Essex* escapes as the kamikaze crashes just off her port bow.

Franklin hit

19 March was a disastrous day for the Fast Carriers. Around 7am the *Wasp* was hit by a bomb which started large fires and killed 102 men, plus injuring another 269.

At the very same time, the *Franklin* was hit by 2 bombs which ignited aircraft loaded with bombs, rockets and gas. This picture was taken by the light cruiser *Santa Fe* as she approaches the burning *Franklin*.

1 The *Santa Fe* alongside the heavily listing *Franklin*.

2 The *Franklin* is covered with smoke as the *Santa Fe* pulls away. The wrecked carrier was moving at about 8 knots and listing heavily. She is only 55 miles from the coast of Japan.

3 As the *Santa Fe* pulls away for another run some of her men watch the holocaust on the *Franklin*. The carrier's non-essential crewmen are huddled forward to get away from the heat and smoke. This inferno was caused by a lone plane which caught the carrier with its flight and hangar decks loaded with heavily armed strike aircraft about to be launched.

The *Franklin* continues to burn as she now lays dead in the water. Another Japanese bomber came in and attacked the 'sitting duck' but its bomb missed by 600 feet!

Taking off the crew

1 *Santa Fe*'s engines held the cruiser up against the carrier as 833 men were transferred. The cruiser suffered considerable damage, including the loss of the spotter aircraft on the port catapult. Note the 'dented-in' splinter screens on *Franklin*'s outboard quad 40mm guns. The destroyer *Hickox* is rescuing men from the fantail while other ships pulled men out of the water.

2 An *Essex* aircraft took this picture above the fiercely burning *Franklin* with the *Santa Fe* alongside.

3 The *Santa Fe* pulls away from the 'Big Ben' as the carrier lies dead in the water. One third of the *Franklin*'s crew were casualties—832 dead, 270 wounded. Almost her entire complement of aircraft were lost.

   The strikes against Kyushu and the Inland Sea destroyed 482 Japanese planes during the 2-day attack.

Efforts to save *Franklin*

4 One of the few pictures taken of *Franklin*'s portside, as the heavy cruiser *Pittsburgh* pulls in front of the carrier to take her in tow.

5 After the *Pittsburgh* towed her out of danger, the *Franklin* was able to get up steam on her own. The amount of damage to the after flight deck was extensive. As shown in this picture, the carrier has already been stripped of quite a bit of her equipment including the deck edge elevator and almost all of her 40mm mounts.

1

2

9. The Last Campaign

Okinawa, April-June 1945

Landing craft head for the Okinawa beach under the *West Virginia*'s guns.

The last Pacific campaign of World War 2 was also the most desperate. A good number of Japanese still wanted to fight on—despite the total collapse of their European ally, Germany. It was obvious that the military might of the entire Allied world would descend upon Japan by the Fall of 1945 at the latest, but Japan's leaders chose to ignore the writing on the wall and continue their futile and suicidal campaign to sink the US Navy. And suicide was just about all that remained as a semi-effective fighting weapon.

On 1 April 1945, Japanese soil was violated with the invasion of Okinawa. It took several days for them to respond. The first massive attacks against the US Fleet came on 6 and 7 April. The strikes included almost 700 planes. The 'Marianas Turkey Shoot' was tame by comparison.

Unlike previous campaigns where the Fast Carrier Force was able to cover great distances and hit the enemy first, TF-58 was restricted to a 60 mile square area just east of Okinawa during most of the 2½-month campaign. Over 3,000 Japanese planes attacked during that period, with the fast carriers as their main target. Despite serious damage to a number of ships, no units of TF-58 were sunk. The Japanese suffered grievous losses. Over 7,800 aircraft were lost from all causes, and 180 ships, including the super battleship *Yamato*, were sunk. By comparison, TF-58 lost a total of only 790 planes (which were regularly replaced by new aircraft flown in from escort carriers). Although the Fast Carrier Task Force lost no ships, the amphibious fleet off Okinawa lost 31 vessels, the largest type being destroyers (13 were sunk). A total of 124 American and British ships were also damaged.

None of the Allied losses even slightly delayed the Okinawa assault timetable. Their naval power was so tremendous by this stage of war the that it was able to absorb terrific punishment without pausing. However, the kamikaze attacks were unforgettable for those who experienced them. Combat Photographers were able to capture much of the action—sometimes with a shakey, or out-of-focus camera. It is unfortunate that we do not have any coverage of the massive kamikaze attacks on the picket destroyers. Perhaps pictures were taken but neither they, nor the men who took them, survived.

As with earlier chapters, the photography patterns in this chapter are basically similar. Peaceful scenes of graceful ships are contrasted with mayhem and holocaust. The extensive coverage of the kamikaze ordeals of both *Hancock* and *Bunker Hill* point out the emotional contradiction endured by crewmen on surrounding ships as they witnessed death and destruction just a short distance away, while they remained safe and sound, unable to help.

The Last Assault

1 April 1945.
Preceded by 5 days of naval and air bombardment, the landings on Okinawa proved easier than expected. The desperate Japanese defensive measures, both on the island and at sea, were to emerge a week later.

Units of TF-58 off Okinawa. The battleship *Washington* throws spray over her bow as she steams past Admiral Mitscher's flagship, the *Bunker Hill*. An *Essex* Helldiver is coming around to land aboard her mothership. The Fast Carrier Task Force would suffer heavy damage during the upcoming campaign because it was forced to remain off Okinawa, where it could easily be found, instead of being constantly on the move.

Allied reinforcements

Units of the British Pacific Fleet refueling off Cape Engano on 23 March 1945. Designated as TF-57 they would soon be operating off the southern Ryukus in support of the invasion of Okinawa.

Evidently, a US Navy Combat Photographer was temporarily assigned to this unidentified British carrier.

Prelude to invasion

The battleship *Colorado* and her sister-ship *Maryland* take on new supplies of ammunition after completing a bombardment of the Japanese island of Okinawa on 26 March 1945.

LSTs en route to the invasion of Okinawa carrying large landing craft which were pushed over the side and sent to the beaches under their own power.

Hancock men relax on the flight deck and enjoy the sun during a lull in operations on 29 March. Nine days later, some of these young men would be dead from kamikaze attack.

Off the beaches

The heavy cruiser *Minneapolis'* 8in guns watch over circling landing craft in the background during the opening stages of the invasion of Okinawa on 1 April 1945. This was the last and the largest amphibious operation in the Pacific. It included 318 combat ships and 1,139 amphibious ships (plus landing craft) carrying 182,000 assault troops.

As landing craft continue to circle, the battleship *Idaho* takes up her bombardment station. The large ships to the left of the *Idaho* are LSTs (Landing Ship, Tank). The *Idaho*, flagship of Bombardment Unit 4, had been bombarding Okinawa since 26 March, hitting Japanese shore batteries and installations.

The light cruiser *Birmingham* took this photograph as she moved up to her station inshore of the line of battleships. While the camouflaged *West Virginia* stands by, a *New Mexico* class battleship lets go with a salvo in the background. The large landing craft in the foreground are LCS(L)s, converted to support craft armed with 6-40mm guns and 10 rocket launchers.

An LSM(R) fires at Tokilhiki Shima near Okinawa. This medium landing ship was converted to close-in fire support with the addition of rocket launchers and a single 5in gun mount on the fantail.

Japan hits back

The anticipated Japanese air attack materialized on 6 April with the first of an intense series of combined kamikaze and conventional strikes against TF-58. At the same time a sizeable surface force which included the battleship *Yamato* was sighted heading for the US fleet.

Corsair fighters and Avenger torpedo-bombers pack the flight deck of the carrier *Bunker Hill* on 4 April 1945.

An unidentified *Cleveland* class light cruiser under air attack off Okinawa on 6 April. The cruiser is making smoke from her stern while executing a high speed turn.

1

2

Near-miss for San Jacinto

1 The men aboard the light cruiser *Miami* were convinced that the light carrier *San Jacinto* was about to be hit as evidenced by this 3-picture series taken on 6 April.

2 It now seems certain that the carrier would be hit at about both after stacks, as this picture shows that the kamikaze appears to be only a few feet away from the ship!

3 The *San Jacinto* steams on as the Japanese plane crashes into the water, 100 feet short of its intended victim.

The negatives in this series are in poor condition—the marks which appear to be white flak bursts are actually blemishes on the film.

3

On 6 April the destroyer *Newcomb* was hit by 3 kamikazes while covering the heavy ships of TF-58. Her midships was totally wrecked and burned fiercely. Out of her crew of 300, 40 were killed and 51 were wounded. This picture was taken on 14 April, alongside a small repair ship. The destroyer's forward funnel lies on its side on the deck house.

Hancock is hit

The *Hancock* burns fiercely on 7 April as the *Essex* follows close behind her, hiding under the pillars of smoke. A kamikaze dropped its bomb on *Hancock*'s flight deck and then dived into the carrier further aft. While this was happening, the last remnants of the Japanese fleet were being sent to the bottom by a total of 386 aircraft from TF-58. The battleship *Yamato*, light cruiser *Yahagi*, and 4 destroyers were sunk. Only 10 US planes were lost.

Essex men watch helplessly as smoke pours out of *Hancock*'s hangar, While the *Essex* remained unscratched, *Hancock* lost 72 men killed and 82 wounded.

Crewmen on *Hancock*'s flight deck, examining wrecked and burned out aircraft.

The attacks continue

Forewarned by a rescued Japanese aviator, TF-58 was ready for the next big strike, on 11 April. Despite their lack of real success, the Japanese attacks continued.

The No 2 gun mount on the destroyer *Mertz* lets go against a kamikaze as the battleship *Wisconsin*'s light AA guns also throw up a curtain of fire. The ships were photographed from the *Yorktown* on 9 April 1945.

A brief respite

This unique photo was also taken by the *Intrepid* on 10 April. The *Missouri* is alongside the oiler *Niobara*. The large derrick abaft the oiler's bridge was used for hoisting landing craft aboard. The light carrier *Langley* and battlecruiser *Alaska* are in the background.

The expected attack

The *Missouri* took this picture of some of TF-58's screening units under attack of Okinawa on 11 April. The dazzle-camouflaged cruiser *San Diego* is in the center, with the *Wisconsin* in the background.

Essex gunners wait for a Japanese plane to come within the range of their 20mm guns while the 40mm mounts on the island fire away. A Combat Photographer took this picture on 11 April, when the *Essex* was near-missed by a bomb which killed 33 and wounded 34.

The battleships in action

The *Wisconsin* in action on 11 April as seen from the *Intrepid*. Note the burning plane above the battleship's bow.

Kamikaze victims

The *Missouri* was crashed amidships by a kamikaze on the afternoon of the 11th. One of the Japanese plane's machine guns jammed into a barrel of this quad 40mm mount. The kamikaze did very little damage to the battleship.

The destroyer *Sigsbee* with her entire stern blown away by a kamikaze on 14 April. A large section of the deck has been peeled back against the No 4 gun mount—3 men were killed, 75 were wounded.

The destroyer *Hazelwood* on 29 April, after a kamikaze crashed into the bridge and then blew up with its bombs. One of her sister-ships, the *Colahan*, is alongside to lend assistance. The *Hazelwood*'s captain and 45 men were killed; 26 were injured.

Intrepid again under fire

Two kamikazes dive on the *Intrepid* on 16 April. The first one, which is less than 300 feet from the carrier in this picture, just missed and crashed into the water next to the ship. The second kamikaze, in the upper right hand side, crashed into the carrier's flight deck.

1 *Bennington* Helldivers fly over the *Intrepid* as smoke pours out of her hangar. The battlecruiser *Alaska* is off the damaged carrier's port bow.

2 *Intrepid* crewmen putting out the fires caused by the last enemy to ever inflict damage on the veteran carrier—10 men were killed, 87 were wounded.

3 The hole in *Intrepid*'s flight deck was made by the kamikaze's engine. It crashed into the hangar and caused extensive fires which did considerable damage. Three hours after the attack *Intrepid* was able to land her strike aircraft. She then retired to Ulithi.

4

5

Back to Ulithi

4 *Hornet*'s photographer caught this beautifully tranquil scene during a lull in operations on 20 April. The destroyer in the foreground is the *Mansfield*.

5 *Missouri* men salute their fallen comrades as the battleship heads for Ulithi on 8 May. She was to proceed to Guam to become Admiral Halsey's new flagship and then return to Okinawa on the 27th.

Bunker Hill

11 May 1945.
Bunker Hill suffered one of the most damaging
kamikaze hits of the war. Her air group was wiped
out and she lost over 600 men killed and wounded. A
spectacular series of photos of this damage captures
the full horror of a kamikaze attack.

Before the storm

Birds-eye view of Mitscher's flagship, the *Bunker Hill*, off
Okinawa as she would have appeared to 2 Japanese kamikazes which crashed into her on 11 May 1945.

Distant views

1 The *Bunker Hill* burns fiercely as the ships around her begin
to record her plight with a series of outstanding photographs.

2 A *Randolph* picture shows the *Bunker Hill* pouring smoke
from both her flight deck and hangar. The light cruiser
Wilkes-Barre in the background is preparing to come alongside.

1

2

Still underway

Despite her tremendous topside damage, the *Bunker Hill's* engines were able to maintain headway, thus keeping the bridge decks clear of smoke.

The *Bunker Hill* appears to be running for her life as flames engulf the ship. The devastation was caused by two bombs and two kamikazes.

The light cruiser *Wilkes-Barre* goes alongside the burning carrier for the second time. Her decks are littered with debris from her first effort to help fight the fires. Most of the carrier is hidden by smoke. The undamaged planes on the fantail are Helldivers.

Hell on earth

As seen from the *Wilkes-Barre*, the carrier's flight deck is a shambles. Nothing is left of some of the parked aircraft except for their engines and propellers. A destroyer's mast is just visible on the port side, through the smoke.

Close-up of *Bunker Hill*'s after 5in gun mounts. Note the water pouring out of the hangar level door at the lower right. While alongside fighting fires, the *Wilkes-Barre* removed the carrier's non-essential personnel.

Aboard the stricken carrier

Bunker Hill crewmen carry a wounded man forward, away from the flames and smoke. The mangled flight deck next to the island is from the second kamikaze.

The Task Force Commander, Admiral Mitscher, was forced to switch his flag from the *Bunker Hill* to the night carrier *Enterprise*.

1 The utter destruction of the *Bunker Hill*'s air group is evident in this view as the carrier now lists from the large amount of water poured into her to help fight fires. The bow of the *Wilkes-Barre* is to the right.

Bunker Hill's losses were heavy: 389 killed, 264 injured. She was the third fleet carrier to be knocked out of action off Okinawa, but the brand new *Essex* class carrier *Shangri-La* joined up on 24 April to make up for some of these losses.

2 The forwardmost kamikaze and bomb holes in *Bunker Hill*'s flight deck. She has fought her last fight. Although repaired and back in service for a short period, the carrier was destined to spend the rest of her days in reserve before being scrapped.

Okinawa is secured

Okinawa was not declared secured until 21 June, and the attacks by, and on, the fast carriers continued.

On 27 May the Fifth Fleet again became the Third when Halsey took over command.

Attacks on the destroyer pickets

1 Close-up of the destroyer *Evan*'s scorecard. On 11 May the *Evans*, destroyer *Hugh W Hadley*, and their 12 plane CAP (combat air patrol) group of fighters fought a 1½-hour mini-battle against 5 waves of Japanese planes (a total of about 150 kamikazes). The *Evans* shot down 28 planes, was crashed by 4 more, had her engineering spaces blown up, lost 31 killed and 29 injured, and finally had to be towed out of the battle zone. This picture was taken at Kerama, Okinawa, on 17 May.

The *Hugh W Hadley* shot down 23 planes, was hit by a bomb and 2 kamikazes, was racked with flames, nearly capsized, lost 28 killed and 67 wounded and also had to be towed to safety. Both destroyers were scrapped right after the war.

The CAP fighters also performed brilliantly—shooting down approximately 50 planes.

Enterprise knocked out

2 Admiral Mitscher's new flagship was hit on 14 May, 3 days after his earlier flagship had been knocked out of the war. This incredible picture shows pieces of the *Enterprise*'s forward elevator approximately 700 feet in the air, seconds after she was hit by a single kamikaze and bomb.

3 *Enterprise*'s forward elevator pit after the elevator was blown out. The men aft of the hole are standing on a flight deck which has been pushed upward by several feet from the force of the explosion. A piece of the elevator rests at the pit's upper right corner while the remains of a Hellcat are at the upper left corner. The bomb which did most of this damage had penetrated 6 decks below. The *Enterprise* was the last US fleet carrier damaged in World War 2. She earned 20 battle stars for her service in the Pacific, during which she missed only one major carrier engagement (Battle of the Coral Sea).

4 A *Hornet* cameraman caught this distant picture of a Japanese plane exploding over a destroyer and showering it with debris, as evidenced by the number of splashes around the ship. The kamikaze was heading for the *Bennington* (center).

After Admiral Halsey took command on 27 May, he sent the carriers against Kyushu on 2 and 3 June to get at the kamikaze's staging areas. During the naval battle for Okinawa, the US Navy was attacked by over 3,000 Japanese planes. By verified count, 2,336 of these were destroyed by aircraft and ships' guns. A total of 7,830 Japanese planes were lost during the entire Okinawa campaign, quite a few never getting close to their targets. They were either destroyed on the ground or lost operationally, by inexperienced pilots.

Typhoon

The battleship *Indiana* plows through the typhoon of 5 June 1945 off Kyushu, Japan. Admirals Halsey and McCain took command of the US Naval forces off Okinawa on 27 May. They immediately headed north to pound the Japanese mainland on 2 and 3 June. TF-38 got caught by the typhoon because of delayed weather warnings and faulty predictions.

The heavy carrier *Pittsburgh* lost 104 feet of her bow during the typhoon. She is shown at Guam, alongside the light cruiser *Duluth*.

1 The *Hornet*'s forward flight deck was damaged during the typhoon so the carrier was forced to launch aircraft off her fantail (as shown) on 6 June. Long overdue for a refit, the *Hornet* was sent to the West Coast for repairs and modernization. This was the only damage to the *Hornet* during her commendable World War 2 career.

Also damage during the typhoon, the *Bennington*'s flight deck was repaired at Leyte Gulf and quickly returned to TF-38.

2 *Essex*'s camera looking at the light cruiser *Astoria* and the carrier *Randolph* as their AA guns practice fire at target drones.

On 6 June, the brand new *Essex* class carrier *Bon Homme Richard* joined the fast carriers providing air support off Okinawa. TF-38 returned to strike Kyushu on 8 June, which was the last carrier operation of the Okinawa campaign. TF-38 anchored at Leyte Gulf on 14 June for 2 weeks of rest before mounting the final strikes against Japan.

10. Victory in the Pacific

The Allied Fleet in Tokyo Bay, July-September 1945

With the close of the Okinawa campaign it was all over bar the shouting. Spearheaded by the US Navy, Allied military power in the Pacific was awesome. Plans for the massive invasion of Japan were ready, but its implementation would be very costly—many Japanese were prepared to fight to the death and approximately 10,000 aircraft were hidden away throughout the countryside. Their suicide pilots, combined with a fanatic defense of the beaches, were intended to stop the Americans, or at least convince them that the price for invasion was too high. This concept had not worked before and there was no reason to believe that it would work this time either—except to spill a lot of blood on both sides. However, the use of the atom bomb finally convinced even the most resolute Japanese that further resistance was totally useless. They now realized that the United States had the capability to destroy their entire nation without any cost to itself.

The folly of continuing the war was very evident when comparing some of the combat statistics. For example, US Navy and Marine Corps aircraft shot down 9,249 Japanese planes in aerial combat, while losing only 897 of their own. In addition, they destroyed 6,221 enemy planes on the ground, while the Japanese could credit themselves with but 969 (some of which were lost on sunk or damaged US carriers). A total of 25,816 Japanese planes were destroyed by American aircraft (US Navy, Marine and Army Air Force). By comparison, Japanese aircraft destroyed 3,410 US planes. When the United States Navy began World War 2, it had approximately 3,500 planes. By the time Japan surrendered, there were 41,511 naval aircraft.

The photographs in the early part of this chapter vividly portray the freedom with which the US Navy was able to operate off the coast of Japan. The battleships bombarded mainland targets with total impunity. Carrier planes finished off what was left of the Imperial Navy's surface fleet. While US Army bombers turned southern Japan into a blazing inferno, carrier planes neutralized military and transportation targets in northern Japan.

When the cease-fire was agreed to, Combat Photographers followed the *Missouri* into Tokyo Bay and witnessed the historic surrender of Japan on her decks. Every World War 2 history book has reproduced numerous close-ups of the actual signing. For this reason, we have not reprinted any of them. Instead, we have gone in the other direction: the camera never goes aboard the *Missouri* but looks at her while both close alongside and at great distances, with hundreds of naval aircraft overhead.

Japan lost World War 2 because she was not able to out-produce the United States. Not only did she lose the production war, she also lost the supply and training war (Japan was unable to maintain a minimum stock of oil). She could not even replace skilled men on a one-for-one basis, while America was able to make good her losses by over ten-fold. When the end finally came, Japan possessed only a handful of operational surface ships, although she still had a fair number of ocean-going submarines. Had the Japanese fought their subs as effectively as the Americans, things could have been different.

Japan had no choice but to accept unconditional surrender; most of her fine ships were either at the bottom of the Pacific or rusting in the mud of the homeland's harbors. Very few American sailors had ever seen an enemy ship, even at great distance.

The Last Actions

TF-38 continued to strike targets—particularly shipping—in and around the Japanese homeland, until the cease-fire order of 15 August.

Symbolic of Pacific victory, the battleship *Missouri* fires a main battery salvo at Japan during the closing stages of the war. There are a number of famous pictures of the *Missouri* firing her big guns, but most were taken in the Atlantic, during shakedown.

The battleships *Indiana* and *Massachusetts*, with two *Baltimore* class heavy cruisers, off Kamaishi, Japan, on 14 July 1945. They bombarded the Japanese coast for 2 hours—the first time that Allied surface ships had fired on the enemy mainland. While this was going on, carrier aircraft swept over northern Japan, destroyed 26 planes, and sank 41 ships and 70 boats, thereby wrecking the region's inter-island commerce.

1

2

3

188

4

5

The only successful submarine campaign

1 A wolfpack of 5 US submarines are greeted by a PBY Catalina as they head into Pearl Harbor on American Independence Day, 4 July 1945. The score of these five subs was as follows: *Flying Fish*—15 ships sunk at 58,306 tons; *Spadefish*—21 ships sunk at 88,091 tons including the aircraft carrier *Junyo*; *Tinosa*—15 ships sunk at 64,655 tons; *Bowfin*—16 ships sunk at 67,882 tons and *Skate*—10 ships at 27,924 tons.

The arrival of the British Pacific Fleet

2 The British battleship *King George V* on the way into Apra Harbor, Guam Island, on 11 June 1945. She was the veteran of many Atlantic campaigns, including the hunting down and sinking of the large German battleship *Bismarck*.

3 British destroyer *Troubridge* enters floating drydock ASBD-2 at Guam on 28 June 1945.

TF-38 off Japan

4 The recently arrived carrier *Bon Homme Richard* refuels from the fleet oiler *Tappannock* on 12 July 1945. The battleship *Missouri* is also refueling off the oiler's starboard side. During the month of June the repaired and refitted fast carriers *Hancock*, *Lexington* and *Cowpens* rejoined TF-38.

5 *Bon Homme Richard*'s photographer took this dramatic view of the oiler *Tappannock* and the *Missouri* on 12 July. TF-38 was on its way north to strike Honshu and Hokkaido. A carrier fighter sweep had already destroyed 109 Japanese planes on 10 July.

Pearl Harbor veterans

1 Some of the US Navy's old battleships steam peacefully out of Buckner Bay, Okinawa on 17 July 1945. The veteran *Tennessee* leads the *California* and *Nevada*; all three had been either sunk or damaged at Pearl Harbor. The *California* had returned to action on 15 June, after the completion of repairs from kamikaze damage received at Lingayen Gulf the previous January.

2 The Japanese carrier/battleship *Hyuga* under attack at Kure on 24 July 1945. She is smoldering from 10 direct hits and is on her way to the bottom. The white circles around the ship are from misses.

TF-38 hit the naval bases at Kure and Kobe on 24, 25 and 28 July. In addition to the *Hyuga*, carrier aircraft also sank the battleships *Haruna* and *Ise*, the carriers *Amagi* and *Kaiyo* and damaged the carrier *Katsuragi*.

One of the few remaining targets

King George V's sister-ship, the *Duke of York*, off Apra Harbor, Guam on 9 August 1945. While in the Atlantic this British battleship had helped to sink the German battle-cruiser *Scharnhorst*.

The second atom bomb was dropped on Nagasaki the same day this picture was taken. The first bomb had already been dropped on Hiroshima 3 days earlier.

The cease-fire

Two of America's largest battleships transfer personnel on 20 August, in preparation to enter Tokyo Bay. This picture was taken from *Iowa*'s bow with Halsey's flagship, the *Missouri*, alongside. Both battleships had bombarded the Japanese mainland during the last month of the war.

Bon Homme Richard's camera looks across the northern Pacific at the British *King George V*, and the American *Missouri* and *Shangri-La* on 16 August 1945. The cease-fire had been called the day before.

The Victory Parade

20 August 1945.
Nearly 1000 carrier airplanes from TF-38 overflew the Fleet in a massive demonstration of Allied airpower, and a celebration of the victory that power had made possible. The Fleet then began its preparations for the entry into Tokyo Bay.

1 The victory parade. This and the following photographs convey the massive power of the Allied fleet off Japan. A *Ticonderoga* plane took this picture of CAG-87 Avengers flying over TF-38 on 20 August 1945. The ship nearest the camera is an unidentified *Cleveland* class light cruiser.

2 A *Wasp* picture taken on 22 August as the fleet oiler *Atascosa* refuels the British destroyer *Tenacious* and the light cruiser *Duluth*.

3 CAG-87 Avengers and Helldivers, also taken by a *Ticonderoga* plane on 20 August.

4 The battleship *Wisconsin* as seen from the *Wasp* on 22 August.

5 A total of 981 aircraft flew over the Third Fleet during the 'Victory Parade'. This picture was taken from the carrier *Wasp*.

3

4

5

The Surrender of Japan

While the large carriers remained at sea, the battlefleet entered Sagami Bay on 27 August, and after negotiations, on the 30th sailed into Tokyo Bay. The surrender was signed aboard the *Missouri* on 2 September 1945.

Sagami Bay

The *Missouri* steams into Sagami Bay on 27 August, flying a battle flag from both the lower mainmast and the upper foremast. Sagami Bay was just southwest of Tokyo Bay, separated by the peninsula which housed the Yokosuka Naval Base. While some of the *Missouri*'s crew were busy holystoning the paint off the teak decks and polishing the brass, the rest were manning the guns in case of a trap.

This picture was taken from the destroyer *Nicholas* alongside the *Missouri*. Three Japanese emissaries have just been transferred to the flagship to arrange the surrender of the Yokosuka Base.

The large carriers of TF-38 remained at sea while the battleships and some of the light carriers went into Sagami Bay, and then Tokyo Bay, to accept the Japanese surrender. Admiral Halsey kept the carriers on alert in case the surrender was a deception.

This photograph was taken aboard the *Wasp* on 30 August, with the *Randolph* and British *Indefatigable* in the background.

Still on alert

1 With the destroyer *Nicholas* alongside, the *Missouri* leads the *Iowa* and *King George V* up Tokyo Bay.

2 The British battleship *Duke of York* steams into Tokyo Bay with 3 battle flags flying.

The Surrender

3 Small craft wait off *Missouri*'s accommodation ladder on the morning of 2 September 1945. The surrender ceremonies are in the process of being concluded. Fleet Admiral Nimitz signed as the representative of the United States. General of the Army Douglas MacArthur, as Supreme Commander for the Allied Powers, acccepted the surrender.

4 Close-up of the crowds witnessing the surrender signing onboard the *Missouri*. This picture was made from a color negative which had deteriorated to a point where the color was very inaccurate.

1

2

196

3

4

The fast carriers out at sea sent 450 planes to fly over the *Missouri* during the signing. This picture amply conveys the greyness of the occasion caused by the weather, and especially felt by the Japanese. The silhouette of the *Missouri* is somewhat confused because the *Iowa* is anchored directly behind her.

U.S.S. MISSOURI

OVER THIS SPOT
ON 2 SEPTEMBER 1945
THE INSTRUMENT
OF FORMAL SURRENDER
OF JAPAN TO THE ALLIED POWERS
WAS SIGNED
THUS BRINGING TO A CLOSE
THE SECOND WORLD WAR

THE SHIP AT THAT TIME
WAS AT ANCHOR
IN TOKYO BAY

LATITUDE 35° 21′ 17″ NORTH ∽ LONGITUDE 139° 45′ 36″ EAST

This plaque was fitted to the spot on *Missouri*'s deck where the formal surrender of Japan was signed. It is still there to this day. The United States Navy, Marine Corps and Coast Guard paid dearly for this plaque: 56,206 dead, 8,967 missing, and 80,259 wounded.

The Vanquished

After the surrender US inspection teams climbed all over the hulks of the once-proud Imperial Navy, observing and recording. Unlike the vessels sunk at Pearl Harbor, none of these warships would ever live again. All were either dismantled where they lay, or raised and taken away for scrap, although a few of the smaller vessels were transferred to other navies as war reparations.

The carrier *Amagi*

The new aircraft carrier *Amagi* lies on her side at the Kure Navy Yard on 14 October 1945. While the US Navy was able to gain control of the Pacific by adding 25 fast carriers to its task forces, the Japanese were able to complete only 5. The capability to replace aircraft, trained personnel and obtain fuel was even worse. These shortages prevented the *Amagi* from ever operating as an aircraft carrier against the US Navy, although she was completed in August 1944.

Stern view of the *Amagi* lying in the mud. Despite extensive camouflaging, she fell easy prey to repeated US Navy carrier aircraft and was sunk on 24 July 1945.

The battleship *Nagato*

The heavy cruiser *Aoba*

Aoba rests in the mud at Kure during October 1945. She was sunk by US carrier aircraft on 28 July 1945.

This close-up of the *Nagato* on 9 September 1945, reveals that her topsides have been wrecked by US Navy aircraft. Her mainmast and funnel have been blown away and the pagoda tower is a shambles. The *Nagato* finally met her end at the American atom bomb tests at Bikini in 1946.

Looking up at *Aoba*'s bridge, foremast and funnel trunking.

The picture was taken from the rear of *Aoba*'s bridge, looking aft. All of her anti-aircraft guns have been landed. The wide platform aft of the mainmast is the aircraft handling deck.

Aircraft-carrying submarines

Close-up of 3 of Japan's aircraft-carrying submarines at Yokosuka Navy Yard. The large circular openings in the forward part of the conning towers served as entrances to the hangars which housed the aircraft. The outermost sub, the *I-14*, surrendered at sea on 27 August. She carried 2 aircraft. The 2 inside boats are members of the larger *I-400* class which carried 3 planes apiece. Both the *I-400* and *I-401* surrendered to US Naval forces at sea on 27 and 29 August respectively. They are moored against the American submarine tender *Proteus*.

The destroyer *Ushio*

The destroyer *Ushio* at Yokosuka during September 1945. One of the 20 *Fubuki* class ships, she was the only one to survive the war. US planes damaged her in Manila Bay on 14 November 1944. She was towed to Yokosuka and surrendered there unrepaired. This photo clearly shows that her forward twin 5in gun mount had been removed.

At Kure

The carrier-battleship *Hyuga* rests on the bottom at Kure on 12 October 1945. She was sunk by US carrier aircraft on 24 July 1945.

The remnants of the Japanese Navy still afloat, at Kure Navy Yard on 10 December 1945 as seen from a plane belonging to the escort carrier *Santee*. Once the world's third largest navy, Japan survived the war with only a light cruiser, a dozen destroyers and some 55 ocean-going submarines, plus several auxiliaries.

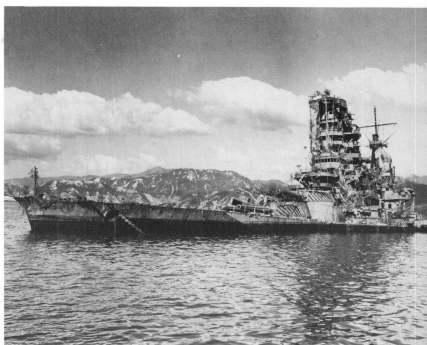

The wrecked battleship *Haruna* at Kure. She was sent to the bottom on 28 July 1945, another victim of carrier planes. Attempts were made to hide the ship through a combination of camouflage paint and foliage. The *Haruna* had been thought to have been sunk early in the war by B-17 pilot Colin Kelly. Instead, she was one of the very last to go down, bombed by US Navy carrier pilots.

Scuttling the survivors

The Japanese submarines *I-156* and *Ha-203* moments before they were both blown up and sent to the bottom off Sasebo, Japan, on 1 April 1946. A total of 24 subs were demolished on this day, all sunk in the same area by TF-96.5 during operation 'Deep Six'. Navy photographers took approximately 100 pictures of this operation. Unfortunately visibility was poor and many of the photos were taken at a distance.

Coming Home

The Navy sent a number of ships home to celebrate the great victory on Navy Day, 25 October 1945, but other ships remained on station to act as a police force. The remainder of the fleet began the process of 'bringing the boys back home'. For this purpose, the carriers proved to be most adaptable, when stripped of their aircraft and filled with Army cots and extra rations. For the *Essex* class carriers, this meant removing their outboard 40mm mounts so that they could squeeze through the Panama Canal.

The *Missouri* goes home

The destroyer *Kimberly* looks back at the battleship *Missouri* on 11 October 1945, while en route to the Panama Canal. The *Missouri* is on her way to Navy Day celebrations in New York City.

The Panama Canal

The *Missouri* drew a large crowd of spectators as she passed through the Canal on 13 October. The Navy Day celebrations on 25 October were the nation's salute to the men and ships of the Navy. It was especially fitting that the *Missouri* was to be open to the public in New York City, where she was built.

The veteran *Enterprise* transitting the Panama Canal on 11 October 1945. Like the *Missouri*, she is on her way to New York City and Navy Day.

It is altogether fitting that we close this book with a picture of the *Enterprise*—the most famous ship of the Pacific War—departing Southampton, England on 17 December 1945. The carrier was packed with 5,000 Americans on their way home.